An Uncompromising Gospel

An Uncompromising Gospel

Lutheranism's First Identity Crisis and Lessons for Today

Wade Johnston, PhD

A project of 1517.

An Uncompromising Gospel: Lutheranism's First Identity Crisis and Lessons for Today

New Reformation Publications
PO Box 54032
Irvine, CA 92619-4032

Printed in the United States of America

Publisher's Cataloging-In-Publication Data
(Prepared by The Donohue Group, Inc.)

Names: Johnston, Wade, 1977–
Title: An uncompromising gospel : Lutheranism's first identity crisis and lessons for today / Wade Johnston, PhD.
Description: Irvine, CA : NRP Books, an imprint of 1517 the Legacy Project, [2016] | Includes bibliographical references.
Identifiers: ISBN 978-1-945500-88-6 (hardcover) | ISBN 978-1-945500-89-3 (softcover) | ISBN 978-1-945500-62-6 (ebook)
Subjects: LCSH: Lutheran Church—History. | Luther, Martin, 1483–1546. | Sin—Christianity—History of doctrines. | Free will and determinism—Religious aspects—Lutheran Church. | Biblical teaching. | Jesus Christ—Teachings.
Classification: LCC BX8018 .J66 2016 (print) | LCC BX8018 (ebook) | DDC 284.1—dc23

NRP Books, an imprint of New Reformation Publications, is committed to packaging and promoting the finest content for fueling a new Lutheran Reformation. We promote the defense of the Faith, confessional Lutheran theology, vocation and civil courage. For more NRP titles, visit www.1517legacy.com.

Cover: *An Allegory of the Old and New Testaments* by Hans Holbein the Younger, painted in 1530.

Acknowledgments

Thank you to the Nebraska District of the Wisconsin Synod and its president, Phil Hirsch, for inviting me to present at its district convention, which began this venture, to Wisconsin Lutheran College and my colleagues for their support, to my son, Ziggy, for the headshot on the back cover, and to all of my family—wife, children, and parents—for their patience and encouragement in my various labors and chasing of windmills.

Table of Contents

An Uncompromising Gospel

Introduction

The defining and most productive ages of the Church's history have been, perhaps without exception, ages of crises. From creeds to confessions, martyrs to confessors, no times have given birth to such rich formulations and testimonies to Christ and His Word as those of great trial or tumult. In such periods, the doctrinal vitality of the church's ministerium, the catechization of the laity, and the confession of the ceremonies of the divine service have played a crucial role in the perseverance of the Christian Church and the preservation of her Treasure.

Why begin a paper about pressing forward with an eye toward the past, though? Times have changed, haven't they? We have iPhones and smart televisions, Google and Siri, a college football playoff. What does the past have to teach us? In addition to humility, a lot. Times change, but people not so much. Faces change, but we're not so different now than we were at the end of Genesis 3. As Calvin put it, the human heart is an idol factory. Its inclinations are still evil, its hopes misplaced. As at Augustine's time, it's still *curvatus in se*.[1]

Nietzsche described those bold enough to move beyond morality, *Beyond Good and Evil*, as "living touchstones of the human heart," and he was more correct than he likely realized.[2] He preceded this with a particularly artful, if unpleasant, observation about Christianity and its constituents. He wrote, "There is usually a stink wherever the common people eat and drink, and even in their places

---

[1]A Latin phrase meaning that we are by nature turned in on ourselves.

[2]Friedrich Nietzsche, *Beyond Good and Evil*, trans. Marion Faber (Oxford: Oxford World's Classics, 2008), 33.

of reverence. Do not go into churches if you want to breathe *clean* air."[3] Obviously, Nietzsche intended to insult Christianity with this observation, but I don't find it insulting at all. I think Christ fully expects His Church in this world to match Nietzsche's description well. He pretty much said as much. After all, the Master sent His servants to the highways and byways, behind the hedges, and wherever the poor and crippled and lame could be found, in order to bring in guests for His feast when the hoity-toity were too busy taking in their clean air.[4] The all too "common" people come dirty, filthy with sin. And yet, that being the case, they most certainly leave clean, their prayers having risen before him as incense.

An account of St. Lawrence comes to mind, when his greedy prefect tried to confiscate the treasures of the church. Lawrence asked the prefect for time to get together and inventory his treasures. He came back the next day followed by a crowd of beggars. "Behold the treasures of the Church," he said, indicating them. You might guess how well that went over:

> In great anger, the Prefect condemned Lawrence to a slow, cruel death. The Saint was tied on top of an iron grill over a slow fire that roasted his flesh little by little, but Lawrence was burning with so much love of God that he almost did not feel the flames. In fact, God gave him so much strength and joy that he even joked. "Turn me over," he said to the judge. "I'm done on this side!" And just before he died, he said, "It's cooked enough now." Then he prayed that the city of Rome might be converted to Jesus and that the Catholic Faith might spread all over the world. After that, he went to receive the martyr's reward.[5]

Whose patron saint is Lawrence? This is one of the fun things about church history—it is seldom as dry as many assume: he is the patron saints of cooks and the poor. That might seem like a bad joke,

---

[3]Nietzsche, *Beyond Good and Evil*, 31.

[4]Luke 14:21–24.

[5]Omer Englebert, *The Lives of the Saints*, trans. Christopher and Anne Fremantle (New York: Barnes and Noble, 1994), 307; http://www.catholic.org/saints/saint.php?saint_id=366 (accessed December 18, 2015).

but I think there is a certain beauty to it. What better thing could a cook do than persevere in Christ and die in the faith? St. Lawrence is a reminder of that. When it comes to making a new dish, cooks have Google for that. They don't need a prayer card. And as for the poor, Lawrence reminds them of the Church's true Treasure, Christ, and that they, though impoverished in this life, like Lazarus, are treasured by Him.

So why all this talk of Nietzsche and Lawrence? The Church is not ashamed of the common, neither of common people nor common things. The Church's treasure was, is, and ever shall be Christ, born in a manger, of whom Isaiah prophesied as though Christ had come a thousand years before, so sure are God's promises: *"For he grew up before him like a young plant, and like a root out of dry ground; he had no form or majesty that we should look at him, and no beauty that we should desire him."*[6] And this common Christ comes through common Means—not with fireworks and a lightshow, but with water, bread, and wine (what could be more common!), and through common mouths on our common faces. Throughout history, the common Christ has used the most common people in even the most uncommon confusions and commotions. And by His gospel, buoyed by His promises, these common people have confessed, catechized, and presided, steadfast, not by any special or peculiar virtue, but by faith, the gift of God. Christ's word was as true for them as it was for the twelve common disciples Christ called as apostles: *"And when they bring you before the synagogues and the rulers and the authorities, do not be anxious about how you should defend yourself or what you should say, for the Holy Spirit will teach you in that very hour what you ought to say."*[7] And what were they to say? My son reminded me of that when he was little. Sunday School was before the divine service at Christ Lutheran in Saginaw when I first got there. One day after Sunday School, we couldn't find him. Eventually my wife discovered him in the parsonage watching cartoons. She asked him what in the world he thought he was doing. He told her he wasn't going to church because it was always the same

---

[6]Isaiah 53:2 ESV.

[7]Luke 12:11, 12 ESV.

thing, "Jesus, Jesus, Jesus." I wasn't happy with him for going home on his own. I was glad, though, that he got the point of the divine service and of the Church's very existence, even if he didn't appreciate it at the moment. He had been listening. That's always a start. So, the question before us today is how we go forth as confessing Christians, as Lutherans—confessing Christianity at its best, that is, in the content of its confession, which is Christ—into a new day. My answer: the same way as the saints of the past, with Jesus on our heads, hearts, and lips, in, with, and under the host for the forgiveness of our sins, and as the reason for the hope that we have for the benefit of our neighbor.

How should we approach this task? We could cover the entire span of church history, but that might take longer than the time allotted for our study. I've instead thought it beneficial to focus on one specific period of history, a critical age for the history of Lutheranism and one pregnant with lessons for our own day. First, we'll examine what exactly Lutheran identity is, as Luther understood it, which I will argue is encapsulated in two of his seminal, and yet understudied, works, namely, his *Heidelberg Disputation* and *On the Bondage of the Will.* Second, we will consider Lutheranism's first identity crisis, the "culture of controversy" or "culture of conflict," as some historians have termed it.[8] This period began with Luther's death and the defeat of the Schmalkaldic League and ended with the Formula of Concord. Third, we will draw some lessons from the Lutheran Church's experience in that crisis and the way it addressed the challenges it faced with the Formula of Concord, which, together with the earlier Confessions included in the Book of Concord, buoyed Lutheranism in these turbulent years and provided a peaceful, faithful, biblical answer to the questions that arose during them.

Contrary to the popular idiom, those who do not learn history are not doomed to repeat it. History is not repeatable. It is certainly

---

[8]See, for instance, Irene Dingel, "The Culture of Conflict, in the Controversies Leading to the Formula of Concord (1548–1560)," in *Lutheran Ecclesiastical Culture, 1550–1675*, ed. Robert Kolb (Leiden: Brill, 2008), 15–64; and Charles P. Arand, James A. Nestingen, and Robert Kolb, *The Lutheran Confessions: History and Theology of the Book of Concord* (Minneapolis: Fortress Press, 2012), 171–190.

instructive, however, and for that reason we do well to give it its due. We confess the communion of the saints and we are the communion of saints. We sing songs those before us sang, pray prayers they prayed, and gather around the same Jesus they gather round on the other side of the altar. We have a God who was born, suffered, died, and rose in history. We stand for the accounts of Evangelists who took great care to include historical detail in their accounts of the life and message of Jesus Christ—they wrote history, very living history. We trust that our ascended Jesus is the Lord of history, acting through and guiding it for the ultimate benefit of His Bride. Church history ought not to have to make its case with Christians. Rather, there are few more Christian tasks than immersion in a past which at the same time becomes and effects our present—it's downright sacramental!

I know some might be thinking, "We confess *sola scriptura*. We have the Bible. Why all this talk of church history and the Confessions? We don't do father theology." Yes, we do confess *sola scriptura*, and rightly so, and yet we do not read Scripture alone, and woe to us if we ever do! Studying how those who have confessed the faith before us have read the Scriptures helps reveal potential blind spots and provide additional perspective. Moreover, we bear historical titles: Christian, evangelical, Lutheran, and so forth. These describe us in historical terms. They demarcate what we confess and what we do not. They are on our signs and in our constitutions, and for good reason. The Confessions are not the Scriptures, and they never claim to be. I challenge anyone to put the relationship between the two better than the Confessions themselves do. Essentially, the Confessions were Wauwatosan before Wauwatosa was cool. They quoted neither seminary professors nor Wittenberg publications as primary authorities. They quoted and confessed Scripture alone as such. The Formula makes this plain, stating at the outset, unequivocally: "We believe, teach, and confess that the only rule and guiding principle according to which all teachings and teachers are to be evaluated and judged are the prophetic and apostolic writings of the Old and New Testaments alone . . ."[9] The Confessions would have

[9]Robert Kolb and Timothy J. Wengert, eds., *The Book of Concord: The Confessions of the Evangelical Lutheran Church* (Minneapolis: Fortress Press, 2000), Formula of Concord, Epitome 1, 486.

nothing to do with parity between themselves and the Scriptures, and we do them a disservice when we act as if they would. Rather, we do well to learn from them, to confess with them, to recognize that our fellowship transcends time and space, to recognize with them the *viva vox Evangelii*[10] and acknowledge it before men.[11] The same is true of those whose confession helped prepare the way for them, who confessed by preparing them, and who struggled to preserve that confession, the confession of Christ and the Scriptures, both in the period of Lutheranism's great identity crisis and beyond, in Europe, America, and the entire world. That's the wonderful thing about the Christian Church: the dead still speak and the living, if they are wise, still listen.

Wade Johnston, PhD
50th Biennial Conference of the Nebraska District
of the Wisconsin Evangelical Lutheran Synod
Nebraska Evangelical Lutheran High School
Waco, Nebraska
6–8 June 2016

[10]A Latin phrase meaning "the living voice of the gospel."

[11]Matthew 10:32, 33.

Luther's Uncompromising Gospel

The *Heidelberg Disputation*

Before delving into Lutheranism's identity crisis, it is important for our purposes to consider two of Luther's most Lutheran statements of the faith, the latter perhaps his most important, alongside the catechisms, at least in the Luther's own opinion. The first is the *Heidelberg Disputation*. The second is *On the Bondage of the Will*. Both clearly, powerfully, and pointedly set forth the heart of Luther's theology. Through relatively brief reflection upon these two works of the reformer, we will also gain insight into the ruptures that developed after his death among those who struggled to define the core and boundaries of this theology and legacy, as well as the best way to preserve the same in the face of external and internal threats.

Nestingen explains:

> While he was fighting his way through the indulgence controversy, early in 1518, Luther was thinking through the meaning of Christ's death and resurrection for the life of the believer. In several writings from this time, but especially in the *Heidelberg Disputation*, he set up a contrast between a theology of glory and a theology of the cross. The issue, after all he had been through, was basic: How do human beings really come to know God?[12]

[12]James A. Nestingen, *Martin Luther: A Life* (Minneapolis: Fortress Press, 2003), 36.

No question could have been more important in the moment. Luther found himself in the midst of great theological tumult. The road from the Castle Church door to Worms was a rocky one. Luther was forced to wrestle with, refine, and defend his teaching regarding Christ and the Christian's salvation. On what basis could he stake his claim to the truth, to be right? The answer for Luther was increasingly clear already in 1518: "I teach that the people should put their trust in nothing but Jesus Christ alone, not in their prayers, merits, or their own good deeds."[13] Nestingen observes, "As he worked his way through Paul's Letter to the Galatians in his first set of lectures on that book in 1516–1517"—there are few works that should be higher on your list of books to read than Luther's later commentary on this crucial Pauline letter—"and took up the Psalms once more, a new theme began to emerge. It is reflected in the different spelling of Luther's name. Martin Ludder or Lutter became Martin Luther, a small change based on the Greek word for freedom, *elutherius*."[14] This theme of freedom was crucial for Luther's later theology, and for the *Heidelberg Disputation*—freedom from sin, freedom from the law as a path to salvation, freedom from a role as an achiever in one's redemption. Luther clearly contrasted the works of man and the works of God. He left no doubt about which brought divine righteousness. One packed thesis after another exploded medieval and innately human notions of some role, even just a little one, in our reconciliation with God. Luther, in short, turned contemporary theology on its head. Out went Aristotle, in came Paul. Out went the textbooks, in came the Scriptures, with Christ crucified as their key.

Luther presented these critical theses at the meeting of the Augustinian Order in Heidelberg, 26 April 1518. This meeting took place every three years. Luther was required to attend as one of two provincial vicars, a job that kept him quite busy in addition to his preaching and teaching in Wittenberg. He traveled with

[13]LW 31:75, quoted in Scott H. Hendrix, *Martin Luther: Visionary Reformer* (New Haven: Yale University Press, 2015), 68.

[14]Nestingen, *Martin Luther*, 37.

letters of safe conduct from his elector.[15] Luther's superior, Johann von Staupitz, arranged for Luther to defend his teaching at the assembly. He was to present the theological method of his university in Wittenberg. As Hendrix notes, "The issue was: How did sinful human beings become lovable enough in the eyes of God to receive grace and forgiveness."[16] Luther's answer was not new, but for most in attendance it was novel. Luther brought Paul's unmistakable answer to light. Critical for his thinking was 1 Corinthians 1:23, where Paul explains that "we preach Christ crucified, a stumbling block to Jews and folly to Gentiles." Oberman notes, "This passage was fundamental to Luther. Already a shaping factor in the exegetical work of his first Psalms lectures, it was frequently referred to later on, and, in the form of theses, presented with all its implications before his own order at the disputation in Heidelberg in 1518."[17] Luther removed the bushel that had been placed over the lamp of the gospel. While a number of the older members of the order were unconvinced, Luther won some of the prominent young Augustinians, including Martin Bucer, who would go on to become a very influential reformer in Germany and England. When reporting about his experience at Heidelberg, having listened to Luther, Bucer said that he was writing "as if in a dream." Moved by the experience, his impression at the time, as Brecht reports, was that "Luther agreed with the (renowned) Erasmus in everything, save that he, in contrast to Erasmus, taught freely and openly."[18] In this, Bucer would later be proven mistaken.

Luther addresses four key issues in the theological theses. Forde breaks them down as follows: the problem of good works, the problem of the will, the theology of glory vs. the theology of the cross,

---

[15]Martin Brecht, *Martin Luther: His Road to Reformation, 1483–1521*, trans. James L. Schaaf (Minneapolis: Fortress Press, 1993), 213, 214.

[16]Hendrix, *Martin Luther*, 69.

[17]Heiko A. Oberman, *Luther: Man between God and the Devil* (New York: Image Books, 1992), 257–258.

[18]Brecht, *Martin Luther: His Road to Reformation*, 216

and the righteousness of faith.[19] These four parts could essentially be broken down into two: our approach to God, which can only fail, and God's approach to us, summarized in Luther's twenty-eighth and final theological thesis: "The love of God does not find, but creates, that which is pleasing to it. The love of man comes into being through that which is pleasing to it."[20] The theses can further be reduced to one key assertion by Luther: *crux sola est nostra theologia*, "the cross alone is our theology."

The *Heidelberg Disputation* stands as a resounding challenge to medieval theology, the *opinio legis*, and all man-made religion. It is amazing that Luther wrote these theses so early in his career and years before the Diet of Worms. Here we find the building blocks for Wittenberg theology at its best and the beating heart of Lutheranism at its most faithful to the Scriptures. Seven years later, Luther powerfully reiterated and expanded upon these themes in his debate with Erasmus in *On the Bondage of the Will*. In what follows, we will briefly consider key theses for each of the four themes enumerated above, and I pray that we will not do so without effect. As Forde asserts, "Thus the cross story becomes our story. It presses itself upon us so that it becomes inescapable. It fights to displace the glory story. The cross thereby becomes the key to the biblical story and opens up new possibilities for appropriating—or better, being appropriated by—the entire story."[21] God grant it: *crux sola est nostra theologia!*

As Luther began his discussion of the first issue, the problem of good works, he drove the lane hard, throwing elbows all the way: "The law of God, the most salutary doctrine of life, cannot advance man on his way to righteousness, but rather hinders him."[22] Down went Pelagius. Down went Aquinas. Down went the little Pharisee in all of us. This is the first bookend of these theological theses, part-

---

[19]Gerhard O. Forde, *On Being a Theologian of the Cross: Reflections on Luther's Heidelberg Disputation, 1518* (Grand Rapids: William B. Eerdmans Publishing Company, 1997).

[20]LW 31:41.

[21]Forde, *On Being a Theologian of the Cross*, 8.

[22]LW 31:39.

nered with the twenty-eighth thesis already quoted above. Out went the law. Well, not entirely, but completely with respect to our conversion and righteousness. What the law demands it cannot give. As he made plain later, "The law says, 'do this,' and it is never done. Grace says, 'believe in this,' and everything is already done."[23] As Forde puts it, "In other words, from the vantage point of the righteousness of faith we see that the law comes up against its absolute end. The law 'finishes' its work in exposing sin and, indeed, making it worse."[24] How does it make it worse? Paul answers that, first, in Romans 5: *"Now the law came in to increase the trespass, but where sin increased, grace abounded all the more, so that, as sin reigned in death, grace also might reign through righteousness leading to eternal life through Jesus Christ our Lord."*[25] Second, Paul shares his own experience with the law later in Romans 7:

> *What then shall we say? That the law is sin? By no means! Yet if it had not been for the law, I would not have known sin. For I would not have known what it is to covet if the law had not said, "You shall not covet." But sin, seizing an opportunity through the commandment, produced in me all kinds of covetousness. For apart from the law, sin lies dead. I was once alive apart from the law, but when the commandment came, sin came alive and I died. The very commandment that promised life proved to be death to me. For sin, seizing an opportunity through the commandment, deceived me and through it killed me. So the law is holy, and the commandment is holy and righteous and good.*[26]

Notice, *"the law is holy, and the commandment is holy and righteous and good."* The problem is that I am not holy. I am not holy and righteous and good. At least without Christ I am not, apart from the gift of faith. That's the whole point of Jesus. That's Luther's chief point. It's not original to him. It's not new—although it appeared so to his

---

[23]LW 31:41.

[24]Forde, *On Being a Theologian of the Cross*, 25.

[25]Romans 5:20–21 ESV.

[26]Romans 7:7–12 ESV.

hearers. It's Paul. It's Scripture. It's indeed the heart and core of all truly Christian theology.

In the early theses, Luther entered into a discussion of categories of sin that might be unfamiliar to contemporary Lutherans. In Roman Catholicism, mortal sin is sin that puts your soul at risk of damnation. The one committing it does so on purpose, according to his own free will, committing a sin that is considered grave—the seven deadly sins might come to mind. Some sins thus become more serious than others, cardinal sins. Venial sins, on the contrary, are sins of weakness. They are not grave sins—minor sins, you could say. The Catechism of the Catholic Church describes the distinction with the following assertions: "Mortal sin destroys charity in the heart of man by a grave violation of God's law; it turns man away from God, who is his ultimate end and his beatitude, by preferring an inferior good to him. Venial sin allows charity to subsist, even though it offends and wounds it."[27] Examples of sorts of sin then follow:

> Grave matter is specified by the Ten Commandments, corresponding to the answer of Jesus to the rich young man: "Do not kill, do not commit adultery, do not steal, do not bear false witness, do not defraud, Honor your father and your mother." The gravity of sins is more or less great: murder is graver than theft. One must also consider who is wronged: violence against parents is graver than violence against a stranger.[28]

Most interestingly, the Roman catechism continues: "Mortal sin is a radical possibility of human freedom, as is love itself."[29] Notice where the Roman Church's error springs from in this instance, as in so many others: free will. Luther would burst Roman and natural human

---

[27] *Catechism of the Catholic Church* (San Francisco, CA: Ignatius Press, 1994), IV. 1855, 454.

[28] *Catechism of the Catholic Church* (San Francisco, CA: Ignatius Press, 1994), IV. 1858, 455.

[29] *Catechism of the Catholic Church* (San Francisco, CA: Ignatius Press, 1994), IV. 1861, 456.

bubbles in *On the Bondage of the Will.* Love—true αγαπη love—is not a possibility of natural, fallen human freedom and mortal sin is the only possibility of it, radical as it is. Mortal sin is not a potentiality for the unbeliever. It is a way of life.

Lutherans reject categories of sin, as if one sin were more deadly than another or more serious in eternal consequences, although we do acknowledge varying temporal, earthly consequences. Luther played on this distinction in Roman Catholic theology, then, when he classified the gravest sins as unbelief and a reliance upon the law for what it cannot give, not because of any fault of its own, but because of our inability to fulfill it. He insisted, "Although the works of man always seem attractive and good, they are nevertheless likely to be mortal sins," and, "although the works of God always seem unattractive and appear evil, they are nevertheless really eternal merits."[30] Once again, the problem is not the law, but us, what we expect it to deliver or how we think we stand with respect to it. The distinction rests, not in the sin, but in the sinner and his disposition and standing before God, whether in Christ or apart from Him. It boiled down to this for Luther: "To say that works without Christ are dead, but not mortal, appears to constitute a perilous surrender of the fear of God."[31] No work is good in God's sight apart from Christ and certainly no work merits or delivers righteousness apart from Him. Rather, "In the sight of God sins are truly venial when they are feared to be mortal."[32] Our best works are filthy rags and the believer will know that and realize that his comfort and security rests, not in what he does, which is stained by virtue of his sinfulness, but in what Christ has done for him.[33]

Luther then addressed the problem of free will—the existence, or lack of existence, of free will in matters of salvation. Here Americans bristle, but we must remember that Luther isn't talking about whether or not we can choose Big Macs or Whoppers, vanilla or chocolate custard, but whether or not we can decide to be saved,

---

[30]LW 31:39.

[31]LW 31:40.

[32]LW 31:40.

[33]Isaiah 64:6.

whether we can choose to do what is necessary for us to be righteous. We need not go into too much detail here, as this topic will be taken up again regarding *On the Bondage of the Will.* Thankfully, Luther made it easy to keep things short. He wrote, "Free will, after the fall, exists in name only, and as long as it does what it is able to do, it commits mortal sin."[34] One might be tempted to ask, "Tell us what you really think, Dr. Luther?" Sarcastic as such a request might be, Luther delivered: "Free will, after the fall, has power to do good only in a passive capacity, but it can always do evil in an active capacity."[35] What a devastating blow to optimistic notions of the capabilities of fallen human beings. It is not original to Luther, though. Once again, Paul beat Luther to the punch in his Letter to the Romans. In addressing whether a Christian is free to eat foods previously prohibited by the Mosaic Law, Paul insisted, "But whoever has doubts is condemned if he eats, because the eating is not from faith. For whatever does not proceed from faith is sin."[36] Whatever does not proceed from faith is sin, and what does the unbeliever not have? So, what can the unbeliever do? And what about the believer, who thinks his works are the fruit of his own virtue or power? He is certainly not acting in faith. So, what are his works? Luther's point is proven. Our will is bound unless freed by Christ and it is in no way freed except through faith, the gift of God through Word and Sacrament. Through these Means of Grace Christ's cross breaks through our self-righteousness illusions and brings what we could never gain through work-based endeavors.

"A theologian of glory calls evil good and good evil. A theologian of the cross calls the thing what it actually is."[37] With this critical thesis Luther endeavored to remove the scales from the eyes of his fellow Augustinians who lived and practiced a disoriented religious life. As Arnold Koelpin explains, "The cross is *the* revelation, and the theology of the cross the only one which deserves the name

---

[34]LW 31:40.

[35]LW 31:40.

[36]Romans 14:23 ESV.

[37]LW:40.

theology."[38] Luther's warning is timeless. Sasse observed of his own day, and it rings true still:

> All Christian churches, also those of the Lutheran confession, must face the fact that as they are today they do not live from the Gospel alone but also from human illusions. It must be clear to us that only a church that is free of illusions in what it proclaims can today speak the Gospel to a disillusioned world—the pure, that is, the real Gospel, and not a gospel that men have fashioned for themselves.[39]

Parochialism, ahistorical assumptions, cultural presuppositions, all such things distract and delude. The gospel must have its way, which means we must get out of its way, or better yet, we must be *gospeled*. In other words, we do not make the gospel our own; the gospel makes us its own.

Few people struggle more with the theology of the cross than the religious. Forde writes, "Religious people in particular seem to have difficulty being theologians of the cross. That is because the theology of the cross is quite devastating for our usual religious aspirations under the wisdom of the law."[40] I am frequently reminded of this in the Ethics course I teach. The course has a wide variety of students, many of them Lutheran, many of them from other denominations, a handful with no religious background. Few struggle more, in my experience so far, with the notion of suffering and the place and purpose of our works than some of those who have been raised in the Lutheran Church. How could God allow us to suffer? Why wouldn't God want us to be a good person? Of course, God allows us to suffer because we live in a fallen world, and He uses that suffering for our good, as He used Christ's, because He is loving, merciful, and

---

[38]A. J. Koelpin, "Luther's Theology of the Cross," 6. http://www.wlsessays.net/bitstream/handle/123456789/2604/Luther%27s%20Theology%20of%20the%20Cross.pdf?sequence=1&isAllowed=y (accessed December 21, 2015).

[39]Herman Sasse, *We Confess Anthology* (We Confess: Jesus Christ), trans. Norman Nagel (Saint Louis: Concordia Publishing House, 1999), 38.

[40]Forde, *On Being a Theologian of the Cross*, 92.

wise. Of course, God wants us to do good works, but we do so, not to be good people, but because we are His people. We are good because He declares us good, because He has planted and waters us in Holy Baptism. Our works are fruits, not seeds. This runs counter to all that is most instinctive and intuitive for us as fallen humans, and so Forde writes, "Religiously we like to look on ourselves as potential spiritual athletes desperately trying to make God's team, having perhaps just a little problem or two with the training rules."[41] Perhaps you don't have that struggle. Good for you. We'll ring the church bells, sing a *Sanctus*, and parade you throughout town later. The rest of us have to settle on promised sainthood, a gift and not a reward—and, to be fair, we should want to have it no other way, because that is how God has arranged it. Baptism, we do well to remember, is not a quick bath: "Baptism teaches a crucial truth about justification. It is not exoneration, improvement, alteration, or cleaning off of the old Adam. David's new heart is not a *change* of heart, but a creation *ex nihilo*."[42] A scene from Bo Giertz's *Hammer of God* comes to mind, a discussion between an old, tried and true, orthodox dean of the parish and his new curate, Fridfeldt, who means well, but has been bitten by the bug of pietism.

> "I just want you to know from the beginning, sir, that I am a believer," [Fridfeldt] said. His voice was a bit harsh.
>
> He saw a gleam in the old man's eyes which he could not quite interpret. Was approval indicated, or did he have something up his sleeve?
>
> The rector put the lamp back on the table, puffed at his pipe, and looked at the young man a moment before he spoke.
>
> "So, you are a believer, I'm glad to hear that. What do you believe in?"
>
> Fridfeldt stared dumbfounded at his superior. Was he jesting with him?
>
> "But, sir, I am simply saying that I am a believer."
>
> "Yes, I hear that, my boy. But what is it that you believe in?"

---

41 Forde, *On Being a Theologian of the Cross*, 92.

42 Steven D. Paulson, *Lutheran Theology* (New York: T&T Clark International, 2011), 157.

> Fridfeldt was almost speechless.
>
> "But don't you know, sir, what it means to be a believer?"
>
> "That is a word which can stand for things that differ greatly, my boy. I ask only what it is that *you* believe in."
>
> "In Jesus, of course," answered Fridfeldt, raising his voice. "I mean—I mean that I have given him my heart."
>
> The older man's face became suddenly as solemn as the grave.
>
> "Do you consider *that* something to give him?"
>
> By this time, Fridfeldt was almost in tears.
>
> "But sir, if you do not give your heart to Jesus, you cannot be saved."
>
> "You are right, my boy. And it is just as true that, if you think you are saved because you give Jesus your heart, you will not be saved, You see, my boy," he continued reassuringly, as he continued to look at the young pastor's face, in which uncertainty and resentment were show in a struggle for the upper hand, "it is *one thing* to choose Jesus as one's Lord and Savior, to give him one's heart and commit oneself to him, and that he now accepts one into his little flock; it is a very different thing to believe in him as a Redeemer of sinners, of whom one is chief. One does not choose a Redeemer for oneself, you understand, nor give one's heart to him. The heart is a rusty old can on a junk heap. A fine birthday gift, indeed! But a wonderful Lord passes by, and has mercy on the wretched tin can, sticks his walking cane through it, and rescues it from the junk pile and takes it home with him. That is how it is."[43]

The dean wanted to free his new, young curate from the bondage of the law, from works as a last resort for righteousness. He wanted to set him free. Rather, he wanted the Holy Spirit to do so, through the gospel. This is the true freedom of the theologian of the cross. He doesn't have to move the peas and mashed potatoes around on his plate in the hopes of a better dinner. He doesn't have to try to conjure up something in himself that isn't there. He doesn't need to find himself, transform himself, or reinvent himself. God makes him new, and in that is peace, comfort, hope, and, yes, true love, which can only overflow into the lives of others as well.

---

[43]Bo Giertz, *The Hammer of God*, trans. Clifford Ansgar Nelson and Hans Andrae (Minneapolis: Augsburg Books, 2005), 122–123.

Paulson writes, "The theologian of glory looks at sin upon himself, forgets all about Christ, and goes back to the law as the means of ridding himself of the thing."[44] Growing up, it was a big deal when my parents finally trusted my brother and me to stay home alone. We lived in a little starter home at that time—we were starting for decades. One house was pretty much on top of another in the neighborhood. When my parents finally decided we could handle things at home without them, we squandered our opportunity to demonstrate our trustworthiness. Some friends came over and we had a regular WrestleMania in the living room. The neighbors told my parents they saw one of us flying across the room like "Superfly" Jimmy Snuka. In the process of our fun, we knocked over a plant. There was dirt everywhere. We got the bright idea to try to vacuum it up. We only pushed the dirt deeper into the relatively new carpeting. My friends started to realize the trouble we were going to be in when my parents got home. Some scattered in terror. Some frantically helped us try to clean up the dirt with wet clothes—once again, a terrible idea. Needless to say, we got so caught up with the stain on the floor that we only made it worse. Rather than placing our hope in our parents' forgiveness—they did *have* to love us, after all—we dug our hole deeper. We were like theologians of glory when it comes to sin. If only we'd have had a theologian of the cross for a friend to stop us and say, "That's a stain, and it's going to stay a stain no matter what you do. You can't fix it. Someone else has to do it for you."

"To be made a theologian of the cross rather than glory is always a shock. Faith that receives the communicated blessings of Christ's victory does not see or feel those benefits. Faith therefore teaches us to believe against our feelings, and only in the promise."[45] Promises are funny things, though. We often take them as might-bes. They *might* come true. The Israelites struggled with this, as do we. In the midst of temptation and suffering we can start to panic. We look around us and we look within. Like Abraham with Hagar, we want to help God's promise along. God's promise needs no help, though—He will countenance absolutely nothing of the sort.

---

[44]Paulson, *Lutheran Theology*, 145.

[45]Paulson, *Lutheran Theology*, 141.

Deutschlander reminds us of so many of God's Old Testament promises, "They are written in the past tense, as though the work of Jesus had already taken place! They and the other promises of the Savior are written in the past tense because his work described there *must* take place; God willed it, and it could not fail to take place just as he said."[46] Yes, God's will is a stubborn thing, and thank Him for that. Luther recognized that, as we will see in *On the Bondage of the Will.* God's promise is as sure and reliable as His person, and there is no better reminder of how reliable His person is than His body on a cross. The crucifix looms large. We live lives of the cross—Christ's cross and our crosses. Luther argued, "He deserves to be a called a theologian, however, who comprehends the visible and manifest things of God seen through suffering and the cross."[47] The cross is our lens. It adjusts our vision and focuses our eyes. It turns us outside ourselves. It finds hope, not in what we might do, but in what God has done, and what He promises to do, which is as good as done. As Luther insisted earlier, "It is certain that a man must utterly despair of his own ability before he is prepared to receive the grace of Christ."[48] Pastors, Luther's Sacristy Prayer might come to mind:

> Lord God, You have appointed me as a Bishop and Pastor in Your Church, but you see how unsuited I am to meet so great and difficult a task. If I had lacked Your help, I would have ruined everything long ago. Therefore, I call upon You: I wish to devote my mouth and my heart to you; I shall teach the people. I myself will learn and ponder diligently upon Your Word. Use me as Your instrument—but do not forsake me, for if ever I should be on my own, I would easily wreck it all.[49]

---

[46]Daniel M. Deutschlander, *The Narrow Lutheran Middle: Following the Scriptural Road* (Milwaukee: Northwestern Publishing House, 2011), 101.

[47]LW 31:40.

[48]LW 31:40.

[49]http://www.iclnet.org/pub/resources/text/wittenberg/prayers/sacristy.txt (accessed December 23, 2015).

One of the most important insights Luther had was that God is not an idea. God is the crucified. He is Jesus Christ. He is a person. He is. His cross is. His grace is. He is not what we make of Him—sorry, postmodernity! His cross does not have whatever meaning we assign to it. His grace is not whatever we suppose it to be. These are concrete realities and they relate to, communicate with, and come to us in very definitive ways: Word and Sacrament. Oberman writes, "For Luther the disembodiment of God into an impressive idea is one of the Devil's decisive misdeeds. Satan may be no doctor of theology, but he is very well trained in philosophy and has had nearly six thousand years to practice his craft."[50] When we fail to realize this, "God becomes subject matter, the topic about which we talk. But whoever talks about a subject must stand above it, must be 'master of his subject.' Thus all theology, as Luther rightly saw, stands in constant danger of losing the right relationship with God."[51] The theologian of the cross recognizes this and realizes the danger—inherent within us—of succumbing to the theology of glory. Yes, "all that we think and do in the church has to be cleansed by the theology of the cross if we are to escape the perils of a theology of glory."[52] Deutschlander writes:

> Could the theology of the cross be the litmus test of genuine Christianity in our day? The corrupt and counterfeit push aside the whole concept of cross bearing in favor of a joy without it. Fake Christianity offers the Christian an imitation of Christ's glory in heaven, not of his humiliation on earth. The phony and the artificial church turns worship into a spiritual happy hour devoid of repentance, with cheap absolution, with no thought of taking God seriously in either the law or the gospel. And people love it. They still get to be their own god, their own bible, their own source of ultimate truth and salvation.[53]

---

[50]Oberman, *Luther*, 156.

[51]Sasse, *We Confess Anthology* (We Confess: Jesus Christ), 46.

[52]Sasse, *We Confess Anthology* (We Confess: Jesus Christ), 52.

[53]Daniel M. Deutschlander, *The Theology of the Cross: Reflections on His Cross and Ours* (Milwaukee: Northwestern Publishing House, 2008), vii.

That is a thought-provoking and critical question. God grant us the humility and the courage to ask and address it.

This brings us to the righteousness of faith, God's gift to us and work in us, all through and by His promise and faith which clings to it. Our righteousness can only be of faith or it is no righteousness at all—not that which avails before God, at least. "The law brings the wrath of God, kills, reviles, accuses, judges, and condemns everything that is not in Christ."[54] There is no hope in the law nor our works of it. "He is not righteous who does much, but he who, without work, believes much in Christ."[55] Christ is the answer. Christ is our only hope. There is no other way out of the mire. "The law says, 'do this,' and it is never done. Grace says, 'believe in this,' and everything is already done."[56] People need something to believe in—desperately—and there is only one thing that meets that need: the gospel. And God is not a grade school recess captain, picking his team from the most worthy to the least, the most able to the least coordinated. No, "the love of God does not find, but creates, that which is pleasing to it." It is not like the love of man, "which comes into being through that which is pleasing to it."[57] Faith is the beggar's hand, as Luther reminded his friends with his last words, and not like a beggar who plays the drums or dances for change outside a ballpark. No, faith is the hand of the beggar too weary to entertain, too embarrassed to ask, too disheartened to even make any effort at all, his fist clenched tight around some imaginary, absent, long ago lost treasure that spoiled, faded, and abandoned him to discontent and despair. He mumbles to himself the empty promises of a life that once held promise, his mind filled with what wasn't. He sits lifeless in the gutter, cold, crippled, hopeless, head hung, unnoticed by all, consumed by shame and sickness. But what happens? The Savior comes along, tugs at his dirty fingers, prying open his filthy hand, and into it, trembling as with palsy, places all that he has: His very self. Even more, He speaks. He speaks of what is: forgiveness, life,

[54]LW 31:41.

[55]LW 31:41.

[56]LW 31:41.

[57]LW 31:41.

and salvation. And just like that, the beggar is—the *was*, better yet, the *wasn't* is banished; he is a child of God! Christ, like the Good Samaritan, does just that, and any effort to bring our works back into the equation diminishes from His gift and robs us of the certainty of His rescue. "Works performed on the premise that one was going to *become* righteous thereby are not good to begin with," Forde points out. "They defend us against the goodness of God."[58] Christ does not need our help. We need his. Luther appealed to Augustine: "The law (says Augustine) commands what faith obtains."[59] As Paul puts it, *"For Christ is the end of the law for righteousness to everyone who believes."*[60] And if Christ is the end of the law, as He is, death loses its teeth. Gum us all it might, it can harm us none, for we are Christ's, and Christ is ours.

On the Bondage of the Will

Desiderius Erasmus of Rotterdam was a distinguished humanist who had made numerous substantial contributions to the scholarship of his day long before his debate with Luther, significantly his edition of the Greek New Testament, utilized by the great reformers. Born in Rotterdam sometime between 1466 and 1469, he received an excellent education and eventually became a monk, although it appears this was against his will.[61] Well-travelled, he had a sophistication that far exceeded any of Luther's own—to be fair, Luther did not strive for sophistication. The contrast between the lives, sensibilities, styles, and personalities of the two men couldn't have been much more different. Pettegree observes of Luther:

> Luther was a German figure and a German writer. His pleasures—food, music, family, beer—were not especially cerebral, and this was

---

[58]Forde, *On Being a Theologian of the Cross*, 105.

[59]LW 31:56.

[60]Romans 10:4 ESV.

[61]Martin Luther, *The Bondage of the Will,* eds. J. J. Packer and O. R. Johnston (Grand Rapids: Revell, 1957), 13. This is from the historical and theological introduction to Luther's work.

> conveyed in an engaging style honed over many years of ministry and preaching to his Wittenberg congregation. Luther was a thoroughly educated man, but he wore this lightly. His sermons were littered with homely examples and improving tales, drawn equally from the fables of Aesop and the follies of life he observed all around him. All of this was integrated into a style of theological writing that Luther had essentially invented.[62]

Whereas Erasmus held up and imitated the method and style of antiquity's towering figures, notably Cicero, Luther, who was not unfamiliar with such men and such style, created his own. He was a gifted humanist, but he blazed a new path, particularly in German.[63] Erasmus could hardly have been more cosmopolitan, and Luther more German. Erasmus hid his barbs, couching them in nuanced prose. Luther was blunt, so that even his colleague and dear friend Melanchthon, who feared the vitriol with which Luther might attack the great humanist, wrote to a friend after Luther's marriage, "I have

---

[62]Andrew Pettegree, *Brand Luther* (New York: Penguin Press, 2015), 33.

[63]Luther was a lover of learning and in no way devalued the classics. He wrote to a Eobanus Hessus, "Do not worry that we Germans are becoming more barbarous than we ever have been, or that our theology causes a decline of learning. Certain people are often afraid when there is nothing to fear. I myself am convinced that without the knowledge of the [Humanistic] studies, pure theology can by no means exist, as has been the case until now: when the [Humanistic] studies were miserably ruined and prostrate [theology] declined and lay neglected. I realize there has never been a great revelation of God's Word unless God has first prepared the way by the rise and the flourishing of languages and learning, as though these were forerunners, a sort of [John] the Baptist. Certainly, I do not intend that young people should give up poetry and rhetoric. I certainly wish there would be a tremendous number of poets and orators, since I realize that through these studies, as through nothing else, people are wonderfully equipped for grasping the sacred truths, as well as for handling them skillfully and successfully. Of course, wisdom makes the tongues of infants eloquent; but [wisdom] does not wish the gift of language to be despised. Therefore, I beg also you to urge your young people at my request (should this have any weight) to study poetry and rhetoric diligently. [As] Christ lives, I am often angry even with myself, that [these] times and ways of living do not give me leisure for an occasional reading of poets and orators. Once I [even] bought an edition of Homer in order to become a Greek." LW 49:34.

hope that this state of life [marriage] may calm him down, so that he will discard the low buffoonery which we have often censured."[64] Needless to say, Philipp would be disappointed. While some of Luther's commentary might have been shrouded in the lowbrow, it was certainly not buffoonery. He dealt with life and death matters. As Pettegree comments regarding Luther's style and labor as a whole, "But if we look beyond the steaming turds and farting (graphically represented with all Cranach's customary skill), we should recognize the deadly seriousness of Luther's purpose."[65]

Erasmus had been in no hurry to attack Luther, although he had grown increasingly uncomfortable with the path reform was taking. Friends of both men worried that open conflict would only harm the reputations of both. Wolfgang Capito begged Erasmus to proceed with caution: "There is nothing [Luther's] enemies wish more than to see you indignant with him."[66] Erasmus himself was hesitant to take up the task, and yet he feared the repercussions of perceived sympathy for Luther and his cause. Erasmus confided in an English friend: "Even had all [Luther] wrote been religious, mine was never the spirit to risk my life for the truth. Everyone has not the strength needed for martyrdom."[67] A humanist through and through, Erasmus wanted moral reform, *within* the institutions of the church. He wanted what he considered to be a more simple, apostolic Christianity. His satirical work addressed to Sir Thomas More, *In Praise of Folly*, evidences this.[68] Pressure increasingly mounted for him to distance himself from Luther and evangelical reform, though. Schwiebert writes, "What Erasmus failed to realize was that a scholar with his reputation could not remain on the sidelines; he must be either for Luther or against him."[69] Duke Henry pressed him to write against his great

---

[64]Hendrix, *Martin Luther*, 166.

[65]Pettegree, *Brand Luther*, 302.

[66]Pettegree, *Brand Luther*, 229.

[67]Quoted in Pettegree, *Brand Luther*, 231.

[68]Desiderius Erasmus, *In Praise of Folly*, trans. Betty Radice (London: Penguin Books, 1994).

[69]E. G. Schwiebert, *Luther and His Times: The Reformation from a New Perspective* (St. Louis: Concordia Publishing House, 1950), 685.

enemy, the reformer.[70] Erasmus chose what he thought would be a tangential issue for Luther, free will, about which Luther had already written some. The product was *A Diatribe or Discourse Concerning Free Choice.*

Luther delayed in reply. It was eleven months before he undertook the task. The Peasants' War explains some of his tardiness, but one must wonder why, if Luther saw this as an attack on *the* heart of his theology, he wouldn't start scribbling immediately. It is entirely possible that he simply had no desire to dispute with Erasmus. Brecht reports that "on 1 November Luther, with absolute loathing, had read less than two quires and was convinced that it would be an onerous task to reply to such an unlearned book by such a learned man."[71] Melanchthon, interestingly, was the first in Wittenberg to respond, and "he expressed a guardedly positive reaction." Erasmus, he thought, had dealt fairly with Luther in tone and method, although Philipp too recognized that he took up "a central theme of the Christian religion."[72] When Luther finally did respond, however, he exhibited no sympathy for Melanchthon's grateful, positive impression of the Dutch humanist's challenge. Luther wrote largely upon the prodding of friends and colleagues, but what he produced was "a crushing, comprehensive restatement of Reformation doctrine."[73] Erasmus was insolent at the tone and piercing criticism of Luther's rebuttal. Pettegree recounts, "Erasmus, as was so often the case, took great offense at this personal criticism. His first reaction (also characteristic) was to try to shut Luther down with a behind-the-scenes maneuver, in this case appealing to the new Elector John," a staunch defender of Luther, "to reprimand Luther for this insolence." Nothing came of it. "The elector forwarded the letter to Luther, and followed his advice to stay out of the quarrel."[74]

---

[70]Martin Brecht, *Martin Luther: Shaping and Defining the Reformation, 1521–1532*, trans. James L. Schaaf (Minneapolis: Fortress Press, 1994), 220.

[71]Brecht, *Martin Luther: Shaping and Defining the Reformation*, 224.

[72]Brecht, *Martin Luther: Shaping and Defining the Reformation*, 224.

[73]Pettegree, *Brand Luther*, 233.

[74]Pettegree, *Brand Luther*, 234.

Luther felt justified in his approach. This was not an idle dispute about how many angels could dance on the head of a needle—though that dispute was less idle than many suppose. Erasmus had gone for the jugular, whether or not he realized it, and so Luther reacted accordingly. He told Erasmus in his conclusion, "I praise and commend you highly for this also, that unlike all the rest you alone have attacked the real issue, the essence of the matter in dispute, and have not wearied me with irrelevancies about the papacy, purgatory, indulgences, and such trifles (for trifles they are rather than basic issues), with which almost everyone hitherto has gone hunting for me without success."[75] Intentionally or not, Erasmus had put his finger on the artery of Luther's theology. If Luther confessed this, we do well to consider whether we ought to do the same. Moreover, when Luther elsewhere chided Erasmus with the objection that "your thoughts about God are all too human," he reminds us still today that it is not Luther's theology at all we confess, but the Bible's.[76]

From early on, Luther's *On the Bondage of the Will* did not sit well with many, even within Lutheranism. Luther's treasured colleague, Philipp Melanchthon, was notoriously uncomfortable with it. Few, even pastors, read it today with any regularity or particular attention, although, sadly, it is more pertinent than perhaps ever before in an American culture dripping with an obsession with choice, even in spiritual matters. Luther left little doubt about the regard he had for this work. In a letter to Wolfgang Capito, the same man who had urged Erasmus to practice restraint in challenging Luther, he wrote, "Regarding [the plan] to collect my writings in volumes, I am quite cool and not at all eager about it because, roused by a Saturnian hunger, I would rather see them all devoured. For I acknowledge none of them to be really a book of mine, except perhaps the one On the Bound Will and the Catechism."[77] Concerning Luther's composition of *On the Bondage of the Will* and his willingness to play within the tensions of human responsibility and fatalism, Kolb writes

[75]E. Gordon Rupp and Philip S. Watson, eds. *Luther and Erasmus: Free Will and Salvation* (Philadelphia: Westminster Press, 1969), 333.

[76]Rupp and Watson, *Luther and Erasmus*, 125.

[77]LW 50:172–173.

that we find there exhibited "the organic unity of his entire body of teaching."[78] In other words, *On the Bondage of the Will* does not deal with a few spokes in a doctrinal wheel; it rather reflects the whole wheel—spokes, rim, and all—working together and centered in Christ and His gospel. Paulson explains, "Luther's *Bondage of the Will* is actually a devotional, pastoral-care book meant to help people like Erasmus who are flummoxed over their salvation."[79] And this work ought to confound not only Erasmus or men like him at Luther's time; it is an assault on contemporary thought as well. Oberman begins the section of his biography that deals with this debate, "In *De servo arbitrio* (*Bondage of the Will;* December 1525), his polemical tract against Erasmus—and 'modern' men of all eras—Luther took up and emphasized the subject of the distant and present God."[80] If you can read it without some part of you—namely, the old Adam—starting to squirm, go back and start over, because you're not reading it right.

Luther jumped on and returned to Erasmus' skepticism early and often through his reply, and in so doing, he engages the creeping, shallow agnosticism of our own day as well. Luther could not countenance such a skeptical disposition in theology. The Scriptures, like preaching, are pastoral. The believer is to be comforted, not left wanting. Salvation is not a might-be. It is a certainty delivered through the proclaimed Word—through Christ present among us in preaching and the Sacraments. Promises are not potentialities, not when they are from God. Our faith does not legitimize or make real our justification and forgiveness; no, faith, the gift of God, like Christ, like the promise, receives our justification and forgiveness. There is no redemption receptionism (when it hits your heart, then it is really what Jesus says it is). Nevertheless, Erasmus had fatefully written, explaining his dislike of assertions, "And, in fact, so far am I from delighting in 'assertions' that I would readily take refuge in the opinion of the Skeptics, wherever this is allowed by the

---

[78]Robert Kolb, *Bound Choice, Election, and the Wittenberg Theological Method: From Martin Luther to the Formula of Concord* (Grand Rapids: William B. Eerdmans Publishing Company, 2005), 42.

[79]Paulson, *Lutheran Theology*, 222.

[80]Oberman, *Luther*, 211.

inviolable authority of the Holy Scriptures"—and he casts a wide net over just what teachings this might include, including that Mary is the Mother of God, the denial of which would be heresy!—"and by the decrees of the Church, to which I everywhere willingly submit my personal feelings, whether I grasp what it prescribes or not."[81] In other words, Erasmus wanted to be a good son of the Roman Catholic Church, whatever that meant, and whether or not he understood it. This was the motivation with which he wrote. In this spirit, he concluded his work, "I have completed my discourse; now let others pass judgment."[82] In quite another spirit, Luther would end his, "I for my part in this book *have not discoursed, but have asserted and do assert*, and I am unwilling to submit the matter to anyone's judgment, but advise everyone to yield assent. But may the Lord, whose cause this is, enlighten you and make you a vessel for honor and glory. Amen."[83]

As mentioned, what Luther attacked in Erasmus' position on free will is not unique to Erasmus. It is native to fallen mankind. There is a little Erasmus in each of us. This is what makes *On the Bondage of the Will* so critical. Like our Baptism, Luther assaulted what is deeply ingrained in us. He killed with the law. He permitted only an unconditional gospel which is gift and all gift. I get full credit for my damnation. God gets full credit for my salvation. And yet, even as I rejoice in God's grace, part of me—once again, the old, sinful part—grates at the notion that my will, that *I*, can't do something, even a little thing, tiny as can be. As I complained to Pastor Vertz when he catechized me as an adult convert to Lutheranism, "It's too easy!" That's why it's no coincidence that Nicolaus Amsdorf, cognizant of dissonance within Lutheranism, even between the teaching of Luther and Melanchthon (and his *Loci*), already in 1534 published his correspondence with Luther regarding Erasmus of Rotterdam.[84] As the human will started to peek its congested, sniveling nose into the tent of our conversion again, Amsdorf was confident Luther's

[81]Rupp and Watson, *Luther and Erasmus*, 37, 40.

[82]Rupp and Watson, *Luther and Erasmus*, 97.

[83]Rupp and Watson, *Luther and Erasmus*, 334.

[84]Nicolaus von Amsdorff, *Epistolae Nicolai Amsdorfii et Martini Lutheri de Erasmo Roterodamo* (Wittenberg, 1534).

exchange was the antidote, even for so prominent a Lutheran as Philipp Melanchthon.

Melanchthon's addition of the human will as a third "cause" in conversion, after the Word and the Spirit, was highly troubling for Amsdorf, the Gnesio-Lutherans, and all who held to Luther's teaching regarding our lack of free will in things above us, in matters pertaining to salvation. This addition was reflective of a general shift in the *Loci*, originally composed as "a guide to reading Romans and thus an aid for teaching biblical doctrine in general." Melanchthon instead developed "a new way of using the traditional medieval schema for organizing questions regarding the teaching of Scripture, according to the methods Melanchthon had learned to use among the humanists."[85] In other words, the *Loci* lost some of their Pauline edge.[86] In line with this, rather than rooting the question of the free will in election, as Luther had (and as the Synodical Conference did in the Election Controversy), Melanchthon began to root it in obedience to the law, a reaction to the sorry state of the churches in Saxony uncovered in the visitations of 1527 and 1528.[87] In so doing, he drew nearer (although not) to Erasmus approach to the question of free will (God's commands) and further from Luther's (predestination). Like Erasmus, he wanted to maintain human responsibility and protect God from accusations of cruelty for commanding what man could not fulfill. He did not want God to be seen as an author of evil, since He creates men unable to do good by nature, as Luther asserted. Melanchthon sensed in Luther's doctrine a degradation of humanity, as the will became like a stone or a block, or even worse. The will was not nothing, he held. God did use it, although not as a primary cause, in conversion. It was not purely passive, as Luther insisted, although deeply beset by weakness. In fact, after 1548 he even spoke of the human will's ability to apply itself to grace to some extent, adopting a formula for human freedom employed by

[85]Kolb, *Bound Choice*, 84.

[86]For a contemporary work that strives to develop Lutheran theology around Paul's Letter to the Romans see Steven D. Paulson, *Lutheran Theology* (New York: T&T Clark International, 2011).

[87]Kolb, *Bound Choice*, 85.

Erasmus against Luther. As Steinmitz notes, Melanchthon shifted in his *Variata* from apparent agreement with Luther's doctrine of predestination to disagreement with it, whether or not he said so directly.[88] Luther meant *On the Bondage of the Will* to bring comfort, but such an attack on one of our most basic assumptions, a free will, made even Melanchthon uncomfortable. "Fear engulfed even Melanchthon, who in later life could not stop warning his students against the 'stoic madness' of addressing 'divine necessity' and the hidden God as Luther did."[89]

Melanchthon certainly was no Pelagian, and he definitely did not intend to make salvation our work, but his addition of the will in any capacity in conversion was problematic and alarming. Mathias Flacius therefore appealed to Luther's *On the Bondage of the Will* against him. Regularly employing its imagery, Flacius counseled, "For a sufficient foundation and demonstration of the truth one need only read blessed Luther's *De servo arbitrio*, whether in Latin or German."[90] Finally, in resolving the debates that had arisen during Lutheranism's first great identity crisis, the Formula of Concord, after quoting Luther's *On the Bondage of the Will* as authoritative on the matter of free will, said of it and Luther's commentary on Genesis: "We appeal to these writings and refer others to them."[91] If Luther and the Formula held the work in such high esteem, surely we can benefit from consideration of it.

In HON 201: Renaissance and Reformation, I require the students to read Erasmus and Luther's debate on free will. To my surprise, when they've had their oral examinations at the end of the semester, many have said Luther's *On the Bondage of the Will* was their favorite thing we read. They themselves have more than

---

[88]David C. Steinmitz, *Reformers in the Wings: From Geiler von Kayserberg to Theodore Beza*, 2nd ed. (Oxford: Oxford University Press, 2001), 54–55.

[89]Paulson, *Lutheran Theology*, 67.

[90]Matthias Flacius Illyricus, *Bericht M. Fla. Jllyrici, Von etlichen Artikeln der Christlichen Lehr, und von seinem Leben, vnd endlich auch von den Adiaphoristischen Handlungen, wider die falsen Geticht der Adiaphoristen*, (Jena, 1559), Civ v.

[91]KW, Formula of Concord, Solid Declaration II.44, 552. Figure out a standard, consistent way to quote the Formula and the Book of Concord.

once caught the connection between this work and the *Heidelberg Disputation*, and they are right in doing so. Throughout the work, we hear echoes of the *Heidelberg Disputation*. The seed sown at that meeting of Augustinians now blossomed. And this is not surprising. Schwiebert traces the kernel of Luther's *Gottesbegriff* in *On the Bondage of the Will* already back to his early lectures on Romans and Genesis and perhaps even his Erfurt days. Schwiebert writes:

> His later exegetical studies reveal that he consistently held this view in which the *Bondage of the Will* was firmly anchored. Luther believed that God is a "hidden God" whom natural man could only faintly detect from his five senses. What he determines on the basis of reason is almost wholly wrong. Only by divine revelation does the "hidden God" become the "revealed God," a revelation which reached its peak in Jesus Christ. Beyond this revelation a human being cannot know God.[92]

Kolb writes, "Luther placed his teaching regarding God within the framework of his fundamental distinction between God Hidden and God Revealed, which he developed in detail first in his theses for his Augustinian brothers assembled at Heidelberg in 1518. This distinction formed a basic part of his 'theology of the cross.'"[93] This was a crucial distinction between the theology of Luther and Melanchthon as well as Melanchthon and his followers and the Gnesio-Lutherans. Kolb observes:

> Particularly important for Luther's presentation of the biblical representation of God's lordship was his distinction between the hidden God and the revealed God. Although Melanchthon could describe God in somewhat similar ways, this distinction did not find its way explicitly into his topical summary of the teaching of Scripture and so did not become a constitutive element in the public teaching of his students, as did the topics that organized his presentation. Gallus, however, recognized the value of the distinction and used it

---

[92]Schwiebert, Luther and His Times, 692.

[93]*Gottesbegriff* means "conception of God" and here refers to the fact that He is *deus absconditus*, hidden God. Kolb, *Bound Choice*, 35.

> to warn against trying to plumb the depths of God's wisdom with the temerity of human wisdom.[94]

This was no subtle difference in theological disposition, method, and emphasis. While Luther and Melanchthon shared much in common theologically and both treasured the other, the tension here would become painfully evident after the reformer's death and in the heat of the culture of conflict, after it had festered, unaddressed, perhaps even unperceived, for almost thirty years.

The Gnesio-Lutherans recognized the critical place the hidden God/revealed God distinction had in Luther's theology. They confessed the centrality of God's revelation in Christ and the importance of acknowledging His hiddenness apart from Christ and His Word. Flacius, for instance, could identify with Luther's confessor's counsel to the scrupulous monk, recorded by Luther in his commentary on Genesis 26, as Flacius himself had gone to Luther in the midst of great depression and spiritual struggle and found consolation from the reformer's repetition of the wisdom he had learned from his own confessor decades earlier:

> Staupitz used to comfort me with these words: "Why do you torture yourself with these speculations? Look at the wounds of Christ and at the blood that was shed for you. From these predestination will shine. Consequently, one must listen to the Son of God, who was sent into the flesh and appeared to destroy the work of the devil (1 John 3:8) and to make you sure about predestination. And for this reason He says to you: 'You are My sheep because you hear My voice' (cf. John 10:27). 'No one shall snatch you out of My hands'" (cf. v. 28). Many who did not resist this trial in such a manner were hurled headlong into destruction.

---

[94]Kolb, *Bound Choice*, 144. Nicolaus Gallus was a Gnesio-Lutheran friend and collaborator with Flacius and Amsdorf in Magdeburg's campaign against the Leipzig Interim. He was also perhaps the author of the Magdeburg Confession of 1550: *Bekenntnis Unterricht und vermanung der Pfarrhern und Prediger der Christlichen Kirchen zu Magdeburgk* (Magdeburg: Michel Lotther, 1550). *Confessio et Apologia Pastorum & reliquorum ministrorum Ecclesiae Magdeburgensis.* (Magdeburg: Michaelem Lottherum, 1550).

> Consequently, the hearts of the godly should be kept carefully fortified. Thus a certain hermit in The Lives of the Fathers advises his hearers against speculations of this kind. He says: "If you see that someone has put his foot in heaven, pull him back. For this is how saintly neophytes are wont to think about God apart from Christ. They are the ones who try to ascend into heaven and to place both feet there. But suddenly they are plunged into hell." Therefore the godly should beware and be intent only on learning to cling to the Child and Son Jesus, who is your God and was made flesh for your sake. Acknowledge and hear Him; take pleasure in Him, and give thanks. If you have Him, then you also have the hidden God together with Him who has been revealed. And that is the only way, the truth, and the life (cf. John 14:6). Apart from it you will find nothing but destruction and death.[95]

Deutschlander beautifully drives home the implications of the hiddenness of God for the Christian life:

> It is easy enough for us here to sum up Luther's thought in the Disputation, but it takes a lifetime to learn it, even to become a beginner in appreciating it. Summed up most briefly, it is simply this: In our relationship to God, in the matter of our salvation, we are and ever remain desperate, poor, naked, starving beggars. God is everything; we are nothing. God accomplishes everything by the cross. All that we bring to him is sin and shame, death and damnation. That is true from the moment of our conception. It is true before our conversion and after it. It is no less true on our holiest day than it is on our most sinful day. And the greatest crime and sin and blasphemy of all is to imagine and think otherwise! For as his glory remains hidden on the cross, so the glory of our salvation remains hidden in our nothingness, our sin, our shame.
>
> Even faith, no, especially our faith, is nothing for us to boast about. To proudly declare, 'Well, at least I believe!' is to miss the whole glory of Christ's work and our salvation. For the faith of which we might like to boast is faith created and sustained entirely by the lowly promise in the lowly gospel. Its beginning, its middle, its end, its whole content from start to finish is to despair of everything in

[95]LW 5:47–48.

> me and to trust alone in him, in his cross, in his promise given in the lowly Word and sacraments. Anything else is not faith at all but damnable unbelief.[96]

Amen! Enough on the connection with the *Heidelberg Disputation* for now. Back to *On the Bondage of the Will* we go.

One of the things I try hard to do as I teach *On the Bondage of the Will* is to be fair to Erasmus. Not all of my honors students are Lutherans, but enough are that we can effortlessly and unintentionally become cheerleaders of a sort, especially since Luther's style of writing makes it so easy to do. When I find myself getting a little too undisciplined, however, I see Erasmus. You see, I am an alumnus of Erasmus University in Rotterdam. Thanks to a sabbatical granted to me by the wonderful parish, Christ Lutheran in Saginaw, where I served at the time, I was able to study intellectual and cultural history there. I passed statues of Erasmus almost daily as I rode my bike to and from campus and walked about. His face is implanted in my memory. Moreover, Erasmus espoused nothing new. He was a faithful son of the Roman Church of his day, even if he did take some satirical digs at it. He was a man, like so many, confused about how our will relates to God. That's why Luther's response to him, for all its bluntness, was at its heart a pastoral answer, a reply to a man wrestling with questions and presuppositions not unfamiliar to Luther personally or pastorally. Recognizing that, we do well to review some of Erasmus' chief arguments before delving into Luther's response. In so doing, we will understand Luther all the better, too. Be aware that for the most part we will not engage various technical and deeply philosophical arguments regarding divine necessity as much as a thorough study of the work should (and as much as they do deserve consideration), but will limit ourselves for the most part to those arguments that touch more directly—and less confusingly, for those unfamiliar with the work—on matters of our salvation: how we are saved—by grace, works, or both—and what role our will places.

[96]Deutschlander, *Theology of the Cross*, 127.

Erasmus from the outset made clear that he would play Luther's game, as a gentleman, I suppose, but he was not thrilled about it. He wrote,

> Now, since Luther does not acknowledge the authority of any writer, of however distinguished a reputation, but only listens to the canonical Scriptures, how gladly do I welcome this abridgement of labor, for innumerable Greek and Latin writers treat of free choice, either as a theme or incidentally, so that it would be a great labor to collect out of them what each one has to say either for or against free choice.

Ultimately, quoting the fathers would be, "as regards Luther and his friends, quite useless."[97] As to what sort of response he expected from Luther, Erasmus demonstrated with a backhanded jab that he, too, could insult an opponent:

> Certainly I do not consider Luther himself would be indignant if anybody should find occasion to differ from him, since he permits himself to call in question the decrees, not only of all the doctors of the Church, but of all the schools, councils, and popes; and since he acknowledges this plainly and openly, it ought not to be counted by his friends as cheating if I take a leaf out of his book.[98]

Erasmus then argued that the Scriptures are obscure, that one cannot know for certain what they teach, at least not in many regards. There was room for a diversity of opinions on a diversity of topics. "If [Scripture] is so clear," he asked, "why have so many outstanding men in so many centuries been blind?"[99] It was best, he held, to avoid unnecessary squabbles. Luther, however, went too far when it came to free will, risking falling into the teaching of Manichaeus.[100]

Erasmus did not teach that our will is completely free, nor did he argue that it can attain to salvation without grace—indeed, he was

---

[97]Rupp and Watson, *Luther and Erasmus*, 42.

[98]Rupp and Watson, *Luther and Erasmus*, 36.

[99]Rupp and Watson, *Luther and Erasmus*, 44.

[100]Rupp and Watson, *Luther and Erasmus*, 43.

clear that grace did *most* of the work. There was, however, a place for free choice, and it did do something. My students again and again return to a specific illustration Erasmus used: "Nor in the meanwhile does our will achieve nothing, although it does not attain the things it seeks without the help of grace. But since our own efforts are so puny, the whole is ascribed to God, just as a sailor who has brought his ship safely into port out of a heavy storm does not say: 'I saved the ship' but 'God saved it.' And yet his skill and his labor were not entirely useless."[101] The sailor did something, right? He didn't simply sleep below deck like Jonah. Let me use another illustration. When we moved to Milwaukee, we had to downsize. We live in a small house in a neighborhood of small houses and we have a small lawn, because we live in a neighborhood of small lawns. We figured, therefore, that we could save some money and maybe help the environment a little if we got one of those old-school manual mowers with the blades that rotate as you push. It was a great idea, but it cuts like a blind, pickled barber with dull clippers. Needless to say, sometimes when I mow, one of my little ones will want to "help me." Of course, I allow them, and mowing takes twice as long and an extra beer. When we're done, though, he or she looks at me with love and says, "Daddy, look what I did." What do I say? I'm not the best father, but I'm not a total failure at parenting. I say, "Yes, yes, you did!" And that is a wonderful picture of our sanctification, as we cooperate with God, ever so slightly—not like two horses pulling a wagon, as our Confessions note—in our Christian life.[102] The Formula explains: "As soon as the Holy Spirit has begun his work of rebirth and renewal in us through the Word and the holy sacraments, it is certain that on the basis of his power we can and should be cooperating with him, though still in great weakness."[103] This is well and good, but it is *after* we are saved, not part of it. In no way do we cooperate in or contribute to our salvation. This is above us—*way* above us.

The second key element of Erasmus' argument is that there is no merit without choice, and no salvation (rewards) without merit.

---

[101]Rupp and Watson, *Luther and Erasmus*, 79.

[102]KW, *Formula of Concord, Epitome* II.66, 557.

[103]KW, *Formula of Concord, Solid Declaration* II.65, 556.

He wrote, "If man does nothing, there is no room for merits; where there is no room for merits, there is no room for punishments or rewards."[104] In Erasmus' view, a grace that did not produce merits was an ineffectual grace—perhaps no grace at all. Keep in mind, again, he was speaking of merits with respect to salvation, not fruits of faith, truly good works. Once again, God was to receive credit for this, but we did *do* something: "And the upshot of it is that we should not arrogate anything to ourselves but attribute all things we have received to the divine grace, which called us when we were turned away, which purified us by faith, which gave us this gift, that our will might be *synergos* ('fellow worker') with grace, although grace is itself sufficient for all things and has no need of assistance of any human will."[105] In other words, grace doesn't need our cooperation, it wants it.

The third main thrust of Erasmus' case rested upon God's commands. Erasmus assumes that God would be cruel to command what we can't do, as if you were to threaten to tar and feather me if I don't dunk a basketball—look at me, that's not happening. He asked, "And in fact are not the Gospels and Epistles full of exhortations?"[106] Erasmus placed one exhortation and command of God after another. "Here again you hear the words 'set before you,' you hear the word 'choose,' you hear the words 'turn away,'" he explained.[107] The only thing that could make sense of things was that God wants to "join the striving of our will with the assistance of divine grace."[108] In fact, Erasmus contended, when Scripture speaks of God providing aid it presupposes choice: "Hence, all the passages in the Divine Scriptures which speak of help serve also to establish free choice, and they are innumerable. I shall have won the day if the issue is settled by the number of testimonies."[109] "What is the point of so many admonitions," he asked, "so many precepts, so many threats, so many

[104]Rupp and Watson, *Luther and Erasmus*, 73.

[105]Rupp and Watson, *Luther and Erasmus*, 81.

[106]Rupp and Watson, *Luther and Erasmus*, 61.

[107]Rupp and Watson, *Luther and Erasmus*, 55.

[108]Rupp and Watson, *Luther and Erasmus*, 74.

[109]Rupp and Watson, *Luther and Erasmus*, 85.

exhortations, so many expostulations, if of ourselves we do nothing, but God in accordance with his immutable will does everything in us, both to will and to perform the same?"[110] Finally, he wondered, blasphemously, no doubt, in Luther's opinion:

> Again, as concerns the precepts, if a lord were constantly to order a slave who was bound by the feet in a treadmill, 'Go there, do that, run, come back,' with frightful threats if he disobeyed and did not meanwhile release him, and even made ready the lash if he disobeyed, would not the slave rightly call the master either mad or cruel who beat a man to death for not doing what he was unable to do?[111]

Erasmus failed to distinguish between works done for salvation and as its fruit, or to consider that the problem rested, not with God or His law, but with fallen man and His sinfulness.

Ultimately, this was an original sin issue. Erasmus, like all who assign our will or works a role in salvation, failed to grasp the seriousness of hereditary sin. He saw us as less than dead in trespasses and sins. There was still a little breath, a little light, a little something God could work with, rather than just stink and rot and decay. He betrayed this view when he complained of Luther and those like him, "They immeasurably exaggerate original sin."[112] This explains the seriousness with which Flacius later approached Strigel's attempt to revive fallen human nature from the dead decades later. The devil may have been behind the surplice, as we will find out, but he was also behind any attempt to mitigate the stark reality of the fall and our original sin. As Luther pointed out, "Diatribe dreams that man is sound and whole."[113]

Luther's response was a *tour de force*. It was thorough, brutal, and uncompromising. Several times longer than Erasmus' original challenge, there is too much to cover here, but we will flesh out some

---

[110]Rupp and Watson, *Luther and Erasmus*, 87.

[111]Rupp and Watson, *Luther and Erasmus*, 88–89.

[112]Rupp and Watson, *Luther and Erasmus*, 93.

[113]Rupp and Watson, *Luther and Erasmus*, 185.

key points. Hopefully, they will whet your appetite for further study on your own. It is a worthy endeavor well recompensed.

As to the collating of testimonies and the number of authorities on his side, Luther dismissed Erasmus' boasting:

> Granted, then, that we are private individuals and few in number, while you are publicans and there are many of you; we are uneducated, you most learned; we stupid, you most talented; we were born yesterday, you are older than Deucalion; we have never been accepted, you have the approval of so many centuries: in a word we are sinners, carnal men, and dolts, while you with your sanctity, Spirit, and miracles inspire awe in the very demons. You should at least grant us the right of Turks and Jews, and let us ask the reason for your dogma, as your St. Peter has commanded you (1 Peter 3:15).[114]

He added later for good measure, "Since it is Luther you are attacking, everything you say is holy and catholic."[115] What mattered was not what many men had said, nor what Luther says, but what God has said in His Word, and what He clearly meant by it. "Let Plato be a friend and Socrates a friend, but truth must be honored above all."[116] Jabbing again at Erasmus' mention that he would prefer the company of the skeptics where Scripture would allow it, Luther urged, "Let Skeptics and Academics keep well away from us Christians, but let there be among us 'assertors' twice as unyielding as the stoics themselves," for Paul had made clear that those with faith in their hearts will confess it with their mouths (Romans 10:10), and Jesus had said, *"Everyone who acknowledges me before men, I also will acknowledge before my Father who is in heaven."*[117]

Luther had little use for Erasmus' example of a sailor caught in a storm at sea. We are not sailors doing our best to assist God's grace. No, Luther developed his own striking image. He wrote: "Thus the human will is placed between the two like a beast of burden. If God

---

[114]Rupp and Watson, *Luther and Erasmus*, 140.

[115]Rupp and Watson, *Luther and Erasmus*, 175.

[116]Rupp and Watson, *Luther and Erasmus*, 113.

[117]Rupp and Watson, *Luther and Erasmus*, 106; Matthew 10:32 ESV.

rides it, it wills and goes where God wills. . . . If Satan rides it, it wills and goes where Satan wills; nor can it choose to run to either of the two riders or to seek him out, but the riders themselves contend for the possession and control of it."[118] The question, then, is what god are we under, the god of this world or the true God. How does God take the reins? Through preaching—and here the Sacraments are not in opposition to preaching; they too preach, they too are the Word. God comes and casts off Satan to make us His own captives instead: "But if a stronger One comes who overcomes him and takes us as His spoil, then through his Spirit we are again captives and slaves—this this is royal freedom—so that we readily will and do what he wills."[119] This is the reason for the church's existence. Through it God storms in as a Stronger One and claims sinners as His own. In it He gathers, in a stable, so to speak, His beasts of burden, bestowing on them in their captivity a royal freedom. We are, as Steven D. Paulson put it at one of the free conferences in New Ulm, God's "royal asses." God still rides sinners, even sinners like us, captive, riding them as His own for their own salvation and the good of their neighbors.[120] It is hard to imagine an illustration that could drive home more clearly how God works in our salvation and how we don't, how we are *pure passive*, recipients, and not acceptors, of His grace. Just as Jesus rode a donkey to His passion, so now, by virtue of his passion, He rides us to glory. Once again, we are speaking about our salvation, not what happens after we come to faith. This is our justification—preached and delivered to us—not our sanctification in the narrow sense, that is, our Christian service *after* conversion. This is not choosing Big Macs or Whoppers, this is heaven or hell. Luther drove this home when he wrote of the term "free choice," "But if we are unwilling to let this term go altogether—though that would be the safest and most God-fearing thing to do—let us at least

---

[118]Rupp and Watson, *Luther and Erasmus*, 140. Luther quotes Psalm 73:22 for support here.

[119]Rupp and Watson, *Luther and Erasmus*, 140.

[120]Steven D. Paulson, "A Royal Ass." Paper presented at Lutheran Free Conference, Martin Luther College, New Ulm, MN. November 6–7, 2013. I have a copy of the paper but it does not state on what day it was presented. I attended the conference, but I cannot find the date in my notes, either.

teach men to use it honestly, so that free choice is allowed to man only with respect to what is beneath him and not what is above him." Simply put, "in relation to God, or in matters pertaining to salvation or damnation, a man has no free choice, but is captive, subject and slave either of the will of God or the will of Satan."[121]

Here another illustration is helpful to understand how exactly God works through man. Luther uses the image with respect to the question of how God works even through evil men—which we would all concede He does, working all things for the good of those who have been called according to His good purpose. It is also helpful, though, for understanding the Christian life: God works through sinners, declared saints, for His purposes. Even the good we do is not perfectly good. The Christian life is like baseball. Batting .300—failing 70% of the time—is considered impressive. It is not like figure skating, striving for that perfect 10 by doing everything right. This is expressed in the *simul*, that we are at the same time both sinners and saints, saints and sinners (*simul iustus et peccator*). Once again, I am sort of hijacking Luther's image here, but it is faithful, I am convinced, to his argument and theology. Luther wrote:

> Since, then, God moves and actuates all in all, he necessarily moves and acts also in Satan and ungodly man. But he acts in them as they are and as he finds them; that is to say, since they are averse and evil, and caught up in the movement of this divine omnipotence, they do nothing but averse and evil things. It is like a horseman riding a horse that is lame in one or two of its feet; his riding corresponds to the condition of the horse, that is to say, the horse goes badly. But what is the horseman to do? If he rides such a horse alongside horses that are not lame, this will go badly while they go well, and it cannot be otherwise unless the horse is cured. Here you see that when God works in and through evil men, evil things are done, and yet God cannot act evilly although he does evil through evil men, because one who is himself good cannot act evilly; yet he uses evil instruments that cannot escape the sway and motion of his omnipotence.[122]

---

[121]Rupp and Watson, *Luther and Erasmus*, 143.

[122]Rupp and Watson, *Luther and Erasmus*, 232.

Thus, God used Judas, who was not forced, but was willing to betray Jesus, although he couldn't do otherwise, for God foreknew it. In so doing, God brought about our salvation, although it was Judas who sinned through his treachery. Similarly, God uses me—very occasionally—unforced and indeed willing, although imperfectly, to love and serve my wife as Christ does His Church. He in the one instance uses an evil instrument to work evil, not because He is evil, but the instrument is. He in the other uses a sinner/saint, because He is good, to work good, although the saint remains at the same time a sinner.

Why do I stress this? Why finesse Luther's imagery? I think it is important for us to remember that this side of heaven we can't get rid of our flesh, try as we might. Only the casket will bring that about. And so, we do well to be realistic about who we are and who our fellow Christians are. We dare not be unrealistic. We do a big disservice to the gospel if we give the impression that the church is mostly where you go because you have your ducks in a row, because you've nailed this whole sanctification thing. Most have heard someone explain that they don't go to church "because it's full of hypocrites." A wise professor taught me to how answer them: "There's always room for one more." We should not be shocked when sin surfaces in the church. We should be thankful to God especially in those instances it doesn't. When I was privileged to serve in the parish, sometimes members would come into my office very apologetic, terrified that I was about to lose all respect and love for them as their pastor. They were about to confess their sin. I usually comforted them by saying, "First of all, you're not the first sinner to come through that doorway today. How do you think I got in here? Secondly, I'm not nearly so concerned that you, *one* of my parishioners, is coming to confess his sin as I am that three-hundred-fifty of them haven't been in here in a long time to do the same." The church is a hospital for sinners, not a showroom for saints. The church grants forgiveness, it doesn't give out merit badges. If you want a pat on the back, turn on Oprah.

This is not to say that there is no place for good works, for growth in sanctification. We do need to remember, though, that such growth most often can't be plotted in a clean, linear fashion. Not too long ago a friend posted a wonderful picture of sanctification. It was a man who tripped on the escalator. He kept rolling down, but because he was on the escalator, as he did so, he also got closer and closer to the next floor. Paul tells us that God has prepared good works in advance for us to walk in as the redeemed (Ephesians 2:10), but that walking is something we learn to do. Have you ever watched a toddler walk? It's not a straight line. It's an adventure. The same is true for us. God rides us also in our sanctification, and when we limp, the problem is not Him. And yet He doesn't hop off. He doesn't leave us or forsake us. He rides on, rides on in majesty, even as His lame horse wobbles and waffles, and He is all right with that, and we should be, too. Frustrated, yes. Sorry when we fail, when we fall short, when we, dare I say it, sin, but also confident that the same one who took the reins from Satan has no intention of letting go, for He has died to ride us and He has risen to give us life. Once again, it's not mostly grace, but all grace. We are not a sailor in the storm. Jesus calms storms. He bids His disciples walk on the water. Trouble comes only when we lose sight of Him who comes at pulpit, font, and altar.

As to the question of merit, Luther quickly cast off Erasmus' argument: "Salvation is beyond our powers and devices, and depends on the work of God alone."[123] There is that Lutheran *alone.* In the Lutheran identity crisis that followed Luther's death, it was the absence of that "alone" that drove the controversies that ensued. Luther burst Erasmus' bubble. The world is not full of decent folk who just need a nudge in the right direction, he insisted, no matter how much Erasmus wanted to believe so, as much as we often want to believe so, as is sometimes evident in our well-meaning but misdirected attempts at evangelism. Luther wrote:

> Meanwhile, we blandly persuade ourselves and others that there are many good men in the world who would willingly embrace the truth if there were anyone to teach it clearly, and that it is not supposed to be that so many learned men for so many centuries have been in error and ignorance. As if we do not know that the world is the kingdom of Satan, where besides the blindness we are born with from our carnal nature, we are under the dominion of the most mischievous spirits,

[123]Rupp and Watson, *Luther and Erasmus*, 139.

> so that we are hardened in that very blindness and imprisoned in a darkness no longer human but demonic.[124]

No, conversion is entirely God's work. We are dead—worse than dead, His born enemies. And how does God raise the dead? How does God reconcile the world to Himself? His Word. "Lazarus, come out." "Wade, come out." "You, come out." And what do the dead do when God speaks? They listen. From nothing He made the world in the very same way. His Word is powerful. His will, not ours, is good. As Luther put it in the twenty-eighth and final theological thesis of the *Heidelberg Disputation*, drawing upon Augustine's own similar observation: "The love of God does not find, but creates, that which is pleasing to it."[125] We are like a stone or log of wood in this regard. Luther countered Erasmus, "By [your] sort of method I can easily make out that a stone or a log of wood has free choice because it can move bother upward and downward, though by its own power only downward, and upward only by the help of another."[126] We have no choice in matters pertaining to salvation, and therefore no merit. Erasmus was correct to see a correspondence between the two. He was wrong to attribute either to fallen human beings in conversion.

Finally, and be aware, we are not taking these arguments necessarily in the order they appear in the book (I could make a good *On the Bondage of the Will* "necessity" joke here, but won't), the fact that the law commands and exhorts in no way made Erasmus' case. Luther wrote, "The words of the law are spoken, therefore, not to affirm the power of the will, but to enlighten blind reason and make it see that its own light is no light and that the virtue of the will is no virtue." Luther continued, channeling Heidelberg, "For this knowledge is not power, nor does it confer power, but it instructs and shows that there is no power there, and how great a weakness there is." And further:

---

[124]Rupp and Watson, *Luther and Erasmus*, 139.

[125]LW 31:41.

[126]Rupp and Watson, *Luther and Erasmus*, 175.

> Accordingly, my dear Erasmus, as often as you quote the words of the law against me, I shall quote Paul's statement against you, that through the law comes knowledge of sin, not virtue in the will. Heap up, therefore, the imperative verbs (from the major concordances, if you like) into one chaotic mess, and provided they are not words of promise, but of demand and the law, I shall say at once that what is signified by them is always what men ought to do and not what they do or can do.[127]

Even Moses knew this. He knew his place. Luther explained, "Accordingly, it is Satan's work to prevent men from recognizing their plight and to keep them from presuming that they can do everything they are told. But the work of Moses or a lawgiver is the opposite of this, namely, to make man's plight plain to him."[128] The chief problem was therefore that "Diatribe is so blind and ignorant that she does not know what law and gospel are."[129] What Erasmus needed was to occupy himself with "God incarnate," with "Jesus crucified," for there we find what we are to know and not to know.[130] The problem wasn't that the Scriptures were unclear, that they did not use simple words, but rather that his opponents were not content with them: "What I have observed is this, that all heresies and errors in connection with the Scriptures have arisen, not from the simplicity of the words, as is almost universally stated, but from the neglect of the simplicity of the words, and from tropes or inferences hatched out of men's own heads."[131] God's commands were just that, commands, and they served the purpose He assigned them. As Luther argued in Heidelberg, and as is certainly the case for the law in its first two uses and outside of talk of sanctification in the narrow sense, "The law brings the wrath of God, kills, reviles, accuses, judges, and condemns everything that is not in Christ."[132] The law commands,

[127]Rupp and Watson, *Luther and Erasmus*, 190.

[128]Rupp and Watson, *Luther and Erasmus*, 193.

[129]Rupp and Watson, *Luther and Erasmus*, 194.

[130]Rupp and Watson, *Luther and Erasmus*, 206.

[131]Rupp and Watson, *Luther and Erasmus*, 222.

[132]LW 31:41.

but it cannot give righteousness. Luther had made that plain, too, at Heidelberg: "He is not righteous who does much, but he who, without work, believes much in Christ."[133] Christ is the only answer. Christ is our only hope. There is no other way out of the mire. "The law says, 'do this,' and it is never done. Grace says, 'believe in this,' and everything is already done."[134] This is the lesson Luther wanted to teach Erasmus. He wanted to deliver him from the doubt and fear of a work-righteous life honestly examined to the comfort and peace of our Christ crucified and risen for sinners. This truth, this message, this hope, this *JESUS* is our Lutheran identity or we have no identity worth having. This is our Baptism—nothing more and nothing less. His righteousness, our salvation. His Word, our justification.

[133]LW 31:41.

[134]LW 31:41.

Lutheranism's Identity Crisis

The Adiaphoristic Controversy

While the doctrine of justification is the teaching upon which the church stands or falls, perhaps no doctrine, outside of that, is more relevant or in as urgent need of study for the Lutheran Church today than the doctrine of adiaphora. Historically at least, adiaphora, or purported adiaphora, have frequently betrayed deeper theological fault lines or tensions. Christian freedom is not a get-out-of-jail-free-card, but not a few have played it that way. We would be served well, therefore, if all who tried to play it in such a way would agree to answer one simple question first: Christian freedom is freedom from what? Moreover, we dare never forget the relationship between Christian freedom and Christian love. If we do, our discussions of our purported freedom have ceased to be Christian at all, and we are no different than the so-called epicureans Luther so derided. Christians are not consumers. The church is not a business. Apart from the Means of Grace, which do not change and are not marketable in the least—Christ was not very marketable, either—churches become nothing more than social clubs with a "t" on top, and not very good social clubs at that. The Elks have better beer. Churches become, not houses of God, but dens of robbers.

Matthias Flacius Illyricus recognized this, and when he saw the doctrine of justification and our passivity in conversion challenged after Luther's death, he spoke up prolifically and prophetically. His arguments are especially instructive and pertinent today, as is the article of the Formula of Concord which largely approved and adopted them, Article X. The conflict over adiaphora, or supposed adiaphora, as well as its applications today, will therefore garner significant attention in this section. Most of the other controversies of this period flowed from it and it set the stage for the identity crisis that ensued, ultimately addressed and largely settled by the Formula.

1547 was an absolutely disastrous year for German Lutheranism, one from which it was completely uncertain at the time it would recover. The Schmalkaldic League, a defensive alliance of Protestant princes and cities, was defeated in the Battle of Mühlberg. Philip of Hesse and John Frederick I, two of the most prominent political allies of Protestant reform, were taken captive, potentially subject to execution. Never was Luther's voice more needed, and yet his body rested in the grave. His mantle had, for all accounts and purposes, fallen to Philipp Melanchthon. Melanchthon was no Luther, however. Certainly as brilliant, he lacked the personality. He did not have the same piercing eyes and prophetic voice. Complicating matters, the University of Wittenberg, along with the elector's title and lands, now belonged to his traitorous cousin Moritz of Saxony. Moritz, called the Judas of Meissen by many, had allied with the emperor to defeat John Frederick and Philip of Hesse. He was a Lutheran, and he had been assured that he would not be expected, let alone forced, to renounce his faith by the emperor. But, he had greatly weakened the stability of Lutheranism within Germany by his actions. As Lutheranism's most prominent prince, now his subjects, let alone his opponents in Magdeburg, had every reason to doubt the extent to which he could be counted upon to preserve the Word of God and Luther's teaching. These were dark days.

When the more prominent Wittenbergers failed to speak up in the face of such challenges and coercive imperial mandates, a man as good as nameless, a Hebrew instructor in Wittenberg, Matthias Flacius Illyricus, did. No one wrote more or so influentially in the Interim Crisis. The Augsburg Interim came first—its city of origin certainly poured salt in Protestant wounds, as it was there the chief confession of the Evangelical Lutheran Church had first been presented. Charles V, riding the momentum of his military successes, reinstated, or attempted to reinstate, Roman Catholic theology and practice. He planned to proceed incrementally, but the increments were hardly slight. Published May 15, 1548, the Interim mandated a restoration of a wide range of Roman Catholic liturgical practices like episcopal ordination, the majority of the canon of the Mass, last rites, the seven sacraments, etc. Lutherans retained Communion in both kinds and the right to marry, but not much else. The Interim reinstituted the jurisdiction of bishops and included doctrinal articles that were ambiguous at best and outright denials of Luther's teaching at worst.[135] On justification it stated: "Since, just as through sharing his righteousness he produces inherent righteousness in the one with whom he shares it, so also he increases it, so that it is renewed from day to day, until that person is fully perfected in the eternal fatherland. . . . Thus, Christ's merits and inherent righteousness come together, and we are renewed in them by the gift of love"[136]

The Augsburg Interim was received with hostility, even among some Roman Catholics concerned for the maintenance of peace. Melanchthon vocally opposed it. Amsdorf dissected it piece by piece—the beginning of Magdeburg's resistance. It was only with the threat of force and the exile of numerous pastors that it was enforced in parts of southern Germany, closer to the emperor's stronghold in the Low Countries and occupied by Spanish and Italian troops. A number of imperial cities like Nuremberg lost much of their autonomy. On the whole, northern German cities and territories fared better. Enforcement was more rare and resistance more vocal.

Moritz did not want to rock the boat in his new territories, where he was understandably very unpopular already, but he also didn't want to risk upsetting the emperor. He sought a compromise. He set his newly acquired Wittenberg scholars to work on a middling formula. Melanchthon certainly did not savor the task, but undertook it without a fight. Part of the reason for his cooperation rested in his well-known astrological interests. He was convinced that the emperor would die soon, so he thought he only needed to buy time.[137] A proposal was drafted in Leipzig. Flacius, in a pub-

---

[135]Article XIII in Robert Kolb and James A. Nestingen, eds., *Sources and Contexts of the Book of Concord* (Minneapolis: Fortress Press, 2001), 158.

[136]Article IV in Kolb and Nestingen, eds., *Sources and Contexts of the Book of Concord*, 151.

[137]Matthias Flacius Illyricus, *Adiaphora and Tyranny*, trans. Herbert C. Kuske and Wade R. Johnston (Saginaw, Michigan: Magdeburg Press, 2011), 275.

licity coup, popularized it as the Leipzig Interim, associating it in the minds of most people with the Augsburg Interim. The authors of the Leipzig Interim had opposed the Augsburg Interim, and so the Gnesio Lutherans called them "Adiaphorists." "Interimists" were those who had supported the Augsburg Interim. The authors in part justified their concessions because some Lutheran territories had retained certain of the practices included in the Leipzig Proposal, including Moritz' own territory of Meissen.[138] Importantly, they claimed that such things were "adiaphora," "indifferent matters," or *Mitteldingen.*

One of the liturgical matters permitted in the Leipzig Proposal, a vestment called the chorrock, or surplice, became a potent image utilized by Flacius and others as a symbol of the demonic nature of the Interims. The devil was behind the surplice, Flacius warned. "Resisting the surplice meant refusing to betray the church into the power of the state."[139] Kolb, Arand, and Nestingen reinforce this point well in *The Lutheran Confessions: History and Theology of the Book of Concord.* They note, "Precisely this reinstating of long-discarded vestments elicited from Gallus and Flacius a stinging rebuke. Vestments are indeed adiaphora, they observed: it is a neutral matter whether the pastor wears an academic robe or surplice or chasuble. The effect of such vestments on the congregation is not, however, a neutral matter, Flacius and Gallus argued."[140] The Leipzig Interim stung more than the Augsburg Interim for Flacius and those who agreed with him, because it was the work of friends, not enemies. Those who had the gospel had seemingly surrendered it. This was evident, the Magdeburgers insisted, in the article on the chief article, the doctrine of justification, which omitted the word "alone." The vestments were but a symptom of a deeper disease. Flacius sought to treat both.

The Adiaphoristic Controversy made Matthias Flacius Illyricus famous, his name known throughout Europe. He became a lightning

---

[138]Arand, Kolb, and Nestingen, *The Lutheran Confessions,* 179.

[139]Oliver K. Olson, *Matthias Flacius and the Survival of Luther's Reform* (Wiesbaden, Germany: Harrassowitz Verlag, 2002), 160.

[140]Arand, Kolb, and Nestingen, *The Lutheran Confessions,* 201.

Flacius argued that the devil was behind the surplice, since it had been foisted upon the Church without its consent.

rod. Mention of him worked either admiration or hostility. A Croatian became the face of the fight to save the German Reformation. This role came with crosses. He was derided and mocked for his foreign ancestry. Some called him the "Illyrian viper" or a "runaway slav"—a racial slur utilizing a clever play on words because Latin does not distinguish the word Slav from slave. He became the single most divisive figure in German Lutheranism well beyond the time of the publication of the Formula of Concord.[141]

Flacius was twenty-seven years of age at the time. He had been and remained a devoted student of Melanchthon and Luther. No one published more than him in these contentious years. A brilliant propagandist, he framed the debate and shaped the discourse of the controversy. Together with the other Magdeburgers, he helped define what was and wasn't Lutheran. Within the walls of the last holdout against the imperial religious measures, which became heralded as "our Lord God's chancery," he produced pamphlet after pamphlet and furiously republished Luther's works.[142] Kaufmann writes, "No other figure in the sixteenth century, not even Martin Luther, wrote and published so many pages in so short a time as did Flacius."[143]

The pastors and theologians of Magdeburg called themselves "Christian exiles." The enemy was at the gates, literally. Partly because of the stand he took at Magdeburg, Flacius' life subsequently became one of perpetual exile. The cross marked every stage but his grave, as he was refused a Christian burial. One need not read many of Flacius' pamphlets from the Interim Crisis to realize just how deeply he had imbibed the doctrine of Luther and methodology of Melanchthon. He had not wanted to leave Magdeburg. He had been happy there. And his departure stood as the key turning point in his life and

---

[141] Oliver K. Olson, *Matthias Flacius and the Survival of Luther's Reform*, 129. The normally even-tempered Melanchthon himself used such slurs regarding Flacius.

[142] Nathan Rein's recent monograph on Magdeburg propaganda in the Interim crisis takes its title from this popular moniker for the city. Nathan Rein, *The Chancery of God: Protestant Print, Polemic and Propaganda against the Empire, Magdeburg 1546–1551* (Burlington, Vermont: Ashgate, 2008).

[143] Thomas Kaufmann, "'Our Lord God's Chancery' in Magdeburg and Its Fight against the Interim," *Church History* 73, no. 3 (September 2004), 576.

career—one from which he would never recover. Nevertheless, he wrote and taught as a Wittenberger, synthesizing what he had learned there. The fault lines already present in Wittenberg before Luther's death had now cracked under pressure and Flacius sought to preserve the best of both of the city's great teachers.

For all the heat of the debate, Flacius maintained a heartfelt respect and gratitude for all that Melanchthon had done for him. He acknowledged the formative influence Philipp had upon his theology and methodology. Even after all the contention of the Adiaphoristic Controversy he continued to laud the *Loci*, alongside Luther's *Postille*, as a seminal Lutheran theological standard.[144] Dingel explains, "In no other theologian of the second half of the sixteenth century does one find this synthesis of Melanchthon's method and Luther's theology so effectively."[145] Flacius meant no ill toward his mentor. Rather, he wanted to nudge him—increasingly publicly and forcefully—into taking a stand. He was convinced that Melanchthon lost something irreplaceable with the death of Luther: a clear, buoying, emboldening voice. As Melanchthon had often tempered Luther, so Luther had bucked up his colleague. Flacius provided the drafting of the Augsburg Confession and its presentation as an example: "At Augsburg, at the Diet in 1530, some wanted to reconcile Christ and Belial in adiaphora, and if Dr. Martin had not at that time been on guard, which one sees in his letters, which are now in print, we now through our own wisdom would not even have a trace of the truth among us."[146]

---

[144]For instance, see Matthias Flacius Illyricus, *Ein buch, von waren und falschen Mitteldingen, Darin fast der gantze handel von Mitteldingen erkleret wird, widder die schedliche Rotte der Adiaphoristen. Item ein brieff des ehrwirdigen Herrn D. Joannis Epini superintendenten zu Hamburg, auch von diesem handel an Illyricum geschrieben* (Magdeburg: Christian Rödinger, 1550), Miv r. See also Piv r.

[145]Dingel, "Flacius als Schüler," 83.

[146]Matthias Flacius Illyricus, *Eine Christliche vermanung zur bestendigkeit, inn der waren reinen Religion Jhesu Christi, unnd inn der Augsburgischen bekentnis. Geschrieben an die Meissnische Kirche, unnd andere, so das lauttere Evangelium Jhesu Christi erkant haben* (Magdeburg: Michael Lotter, 1550), Hiii r.

Flacius left Wittenberg in 1549, initially leaving his "very pregnant wife" behind.[147] At first he refused the hospitality of Magdeburg for the sake of his health. He was afraid he "would have to eat smoked bacon and meat, and also salted and dried fish."[148] He eventually changed his mind after further travels, to the great relief of the Magdeburgers. In many ways, Flacius would make Magdeburg in so far as it succeeded as the "chancery of God," and yet, just as much, Magdeburg made Flacius. It was *the* definitive period of his life. Together, he, Amsdorf, Gallus, and the other theologians and pastors of the city made their famous resistance and preserved the Lutheran Reformation as they had known it.

In his pivotal work, *A Book about True and False Adiaphora*, as well as the admonitions he wrote to fellow Lutherans throughout the empire, Flacius set forth his argument for what made something an adiaphora or disqualified it from being the same.[149] He established a "General Rule about Ceremonies" to serve as a guideline:

> All ceremonies and church practices are in and of themselves free and they will always be. When, however, coercion, the false illusion that they were worship of God and must be observed, renunciation

---

[147]Thomas Kaufmann, "Matthias Flacius Illyricus. Lutherischer Theologe und Magdeburer Publizist," in *Mitteldeutsche Lebensbilder: Menschen im Zeitalter der Reformation*, ed. Werner Freitag (Köln: Böhlau Verlag, 2004), 183.

[148]Kaufmann, "Matthias Flacius Illyricus," 183.

[149]Matthias Flacius Illyricus, *Vermanung Matth. Flacii Illyrici zur gedult und glauben zu Gott, im Creutz dieser verfolgung Geschrieben an die Kirche Christi zu Magdeburg* (Magdeburg: Christian Rödinger, 1551); *Ein vermanung zur bestendigkeit, in bekentnis der warheit, Creutz, und Gebett, in dieser betrübten zeit sehr nützlich und tröstlich* (Magdeburg: Michael Lotter, 1549); *Eine Christliche vermanung zur bestendigkeit, inn der waren reinen Religion Jhesu Christi, unnd inn der Augsburgischen bekentnis. Geschrieben an die Meissnische Kirche, unnd andere, so das lauttere Evangelium Jhesu Christi erkant haben* (Magdeburg: Michael Lotter, 1550); *Ein buch, von waren und falschen Mitteldingen, Darin fast der gantze handel von Mitteldingen erkleret wird, widder die schedliche Rotte der Adiaphoristen. Item ein brieff des ehrwirdigen Herrn D. Joannis Epini superintendenten zu Hamburg, auch von diesem handel an Illyricum geschrieben* (Magdeburg: Christian Rödinger, 1550).

> [of the faith], offense, [or] an opening for godless develops, and when, in whatever way it might happen, they do not build up but rather tear down the church of God and mock God, then they are no longer adiaphora.[150]

He outlined three grounds for the introduction or employment of adiaphora in the church:

> One should now observe that there are three grounds for establishing adiaphora. The first is the general command of God that he wants to have everything in the church done in an orderly and proper fashion and to serve for edification, inasmuch as he is a God of order and not of disorder. The second is the free Christian desire of the church. . . . The third are the judicious, God-fearing people for whom the church is inclined to establish such adiaphora. This is what may be said about the establishment of adiaphora.[151]

This is not the place for an extended discussion for all of Flacius' arguments or all of the Scriptures he summoned in support of his cause—I know a long thesis by a dubious historian on that topic, if you ever have trouble falling asleep. Ultimately, Flacius confessed that Christians and churches are free, but also bound together in love. He echoed the maxim of St. Paul: *"'All things are lawful,' but not all things are helpful. 'All things are lawful,' but not all things build up."*[152] Furthermore, the state had no right to force ceremonies and practices upon the church. This was a clear violation of Christian freedom and a confusion of the two kingdoms. This was one of the first great birth pangs of the rocky (and sometimes not rocky enough) relationship between church and state in Protestant Europe and Lutheran Germany. Unfortunately, Flacius' concerns did not get lasting attention and the marriage between church and state proceeded apace in the centuries to follow in Germany, giving way to the nigh-confessionless state church of our day, in which all that

---

[150]Flacius, *Ein buch von waren und falschen Mitteldingen*, Ai v.

[151]Flacius, *Ein buch, von waren und falschen Mitteldingen*, Jiii v.

[152]1 Corinthians 10:23 ESV.

Luther and his heirs fought to preserve gets more lip service than love and attention.

The Synergistic Controversy over Free Will

While this controversy played a pivotal role in the culture of conflict that developed after Luther's death, in this study we will pay more attention to the subsequent controversy that developed over original sin, first, because we've covered much concerning free will already, and second, and most significantly, because the controversy over original sin was an expansion and natural offshoot of the Synergistic Controversy. Regarding the connection between the two debates, unsurprisingly, since Erasmus already indicated the connection between the two when he complained that Luther greatly inflated original sin in arguing against free will, Bente rightly observes that "the Flacian Controversy sprang from, and must be regarded as an episode of the Synergistic Controversy, in which also some champions of Lutheran theology (Amsdorf, Wigand, Heshusius, and others) had occasionally employed unguarded, extreme, and inadequate expressions."[153] That the debate over original sin flowed from a debate over free will shows what Flacius and Amsdorf thought was at stake: the very heart and core of Luther's Reformation, the teaching plainly set forth in the work that Luther throughout his life considered to be one of his finest, *On the Bondage of the Will.* "Luther had," after all, "thanked Erasmus for putting his finger on the very heartbeat of his theology: his understanding that the sinful human will is bound and cannot choose to trust God and obey him by its own power and strength."[154]

This struggle over the existence role of free will in conversion was therefore nothing new in the minds of a number of the Magdeburgers, especially the old stalwart, Amsdorf. He had been fighting this battle, although in a more muted fashion, since the 1530s, when he grew concerned about Melanchthon's changes to

---

[153]F. Bente, *Historical Introductions to the Lutheran Confessions*, 2nd ed. (St. Louis: Concordia Publishing House, 2005), 336.

[154]Arand, Kolb, and Nestingen, *The Lutheran Confessions*, 201.

his *Loci*. This was for Amsdorf part of a decades-long challenge to Luther's teaching, confirmed further in the heat of the Adiaphoristic Controversy. In 1550, before the Synergistic Controversy had erupted, Melanchthon attacked Flacius and the Gnesio-Lutheran on the matter of the will, using language that Erasmus himself had employed against Luther. In the preface of a work translated by Caspar Cruciger, Melanchthon warned about "Stoic ravings about necessity and fate," and later he assailed the "fatalism" of those who focused too much on election.[155] This is more evidence that differences of conviction regarding free will and conversion had festered in Wittenberg for decades, long before Luther's death. And we dare not presume that the challenge hasn't persisted ever since. It is only by God's unfathomable grace that here, in the heartland of America, almost five hundred years later, Lutherans gather who are still committed to persisting in this teaching. If we are honest, much of Lutheranism abandoned it long ago, in practice if not in doctrine. Moreover, a number of those pockets of Lutherans who have held onto it by the mercy of the Savior seem hell-bent on following the path so many others have followed. The biblical doctrine of the will is a potent teaching, but never popular. It is divine, but, as Luther warned Erasmus, not at all human. This is simply not how mankind imagines itself. If only heaven—and hell—were a function of our imagination!

Kolb notes, "It is no surprise that when one of Melanchthon's students who had helped formulate the Leipzig Proposal, Johann Pfeffinger, advanced his own version of Melanchthon's doctrine of the free will, he raised Amsdorf's ire, especially since Pfeffinger had been a close associate of Duke Moritz even before the Smalcald War broke out."[156] As we established, this was an ongoing struggle, the fault lines were long there and visible to those who chose to look carefully. Pfeffinger had written theses about the role of the will in conversion to be debated within the University of Leipzig in 1555.[157] Objections were quickly raised, however, and the discussion spread

[155]Kolb, *Bound Choice*, 107.

[156]Arand, Kolb, and Nestingen, *The Lutheran Confessions*, 201.

[157]Arand, Kolb, and Nestingen, *The Lutheran Confessions*, 202.

well beyond the university. Amsdorf saw in Pfeffinger's teaching the forfeiture of all of Luther's teaching and an attack on the very doctrine of justification. Flacius agreed. Now in Jena as a prominent professor, he made his displeasure known. Amsdorf "agreed that the sinful will is active, but it is captive to Satan. In other words, it plays only a negative, harmful role. God calls all people through the gospel, but he draws only those whom he has chosen as his children to himself."[158] The dispute led to a broader concern about Melanchthon's teaching, and Nicolaus Gallus, a partner in Magdeburg's cause against the Interim, led the charge. Melanchthon denied he was in error, but he did concede "that Luther had erred in the same direction as Gallus."[159] There is much in this admission. Bente points back to the *Heidelberg Disputation* in his review of the controversy.[160] Luther's teaching had been clear for almost forty years at this point. *On the Bondage of the Will* was but an extended commentary on what was already present, albeit nascent, in the *Disputation*.

Johann Pfeffinger's 1555 defense of the Leipzig Interim's language in his work *Five Questions concerning the Freedom of the Human Will* flowed directly from the Adiaphoristic Controversy.[161] It was an unabashed defense of the synergism of Melanchthon, at least as Pfeffinger understood and interpreted it. A dispute largely about ceremony had thus become indicative and revelatory of deeper theological issues. Adiaphora may be neither commanded nor forbidden by God's Word, but they are not always indifferent—in other words, they are not always real adiaphora. Pfeffinger's teaching was largely his teacher's. He held to the three causes long taught in Melanchthon's revised *Loci* of 1543: "the Holy Spirit moving the heart, the voice of God, and the human will which assents to the divine voice."[162] It was as a student of Melanchthon, holding essentially the same

---

[158]Arand, Kolb, and Nestingen, *The Lutheran Confessions*, 204.

[159]Arand, Kolb, and Nestingen, *The Lutheran Confessions*, 204.

[160]Bente, *Historical Introductions to the Lutheran Confessions*, 294.

[161]Johannes Pfeffinger, *De Libertate Voluntatis Humanae Quaestiones Quinque* (Leipzig: Gerorg Hantzsch, 1555).

[162]Dingel, "Culture of Conflict," 50.

convictions, that Viktorin Strigel would envelope Flacius in the controversy that would prove the undoing of his academic career.

Amsdorf and Flacius opposed Pfeffinger, and through him, Melanchthon, not to be right, not because they were part of an inquisition, not because they did not love the brotherhood, but because they saw a threat to the very heart of the Scriptures and an undermining of the entire Lutheran Reformation. One's position on the human will's role in conversion and the state of man in original sin reveals what he really believes about how we are saved. Often false conceptions of the two, free will and original sin, serve to flank the chief article and overcome it, even while saying nice things about it. History bears this out and our own day attests to it as well. Justification is not another article in the Confessions. Justification is intimately connected to all of them. We do well to remember that. That was the message of the *Heidelberg Disputation* and *On the Bondage of the Will*. That is part and parcel of true Lutheran identity. Doctrine is not a pizza pie made up of slices. Doctrine is a unity, a totality. That is why our Confessions more often than not speak of doctrine rather than doctrines. Christ is the center of all we believe and teach, and like rays of the sun, all we believe and teach emanates from Him, or is not of Him at all, and therefore unchristian. The same is also true of the relationship between doctrine and practice. Practice confesses doctrine. It shows what we believe and teach. It makes clear how we think God does His work. It showcases His Word or it distracts from it. It trusts preaching—Word and Sacrament—to do its work, or it doesn't. As with Abraham and the promise of a son, God's promise does not need any helping along, just as our will doesn't need just a smidge of nudging in the right direction. God's promise is sufficient, and it alone can take the sinful will captive, can take the reins from the devil. This is not one aspect of Lutheran doctrine. This is fundamental to Lutheran teaching and critical to a proper, Christian understanding of the Scriptures as a whole and at their most basic.

The Majorist Controversy over Good Works

"[Georg] Major's defense of necessary good works was no isolated phenomenon. The controversies of the Late Reformation, adiaphorism, majorism, synergism, Otto Ritschl wrote, 'belong together.'"[163] That is how Oliver Olson describes the onset of this controversy over good works. Reflecting back in 1559, Flacius expressed the exact same take on things.[164] Major was motivated by a desire to defend his and the other Wittenbergers' participation in the drafting of the Leipzig Proposal. Rather than admitting his error, he sought to defend it, and the reputation of Melanchthon, who would nonetheless disavow Major's teaching regarding good works. Luther's *sola* was left out of the Leipzig Proposal. That was indefensible. Lutheranism hinges on that *sola*. The Gnesio-Lutherans were not imagining that the chief teaching of Christianity was under attack. It was right there, *not* in print.

Major built on Melanchthon's teaching, but did not repristinate it. He went farther than the Preceptor would ever have gone. Major argued that good works are not only necessary—a statement with which Flacius, Amsdorf, and the Gnesio-Lutherans could have agreed—but that they are necessary *for salvation*. This claim was not without strategic interests. The Wittenbergers had more than once and without ambiguity painted the Magdeburgers and those who agreed with them as antinomians who despised the law of God. Amsdorf vigorously protested that Major knew full well that they taught correctly in Magdeburg regarding faith and good works.[165] Flacius would have nothing to do with such claims.[166] Coming from Major, though, they bore extra sting. Flacius had considered Major a good friend in Wittenberg. And yet Major had not only made false accusations, but he had done so in an underhanded and most unbrotherly way. Major held both Flacius and his positions up for ridicule, not because he demonstrated that Flacius was an immoral man or that his teachings were false, but on the grounds that he was a foreigner and not ordained. Melanchthon, however, was also not

---

163Olson, *Matthias Flacius and the Survival of Luther's Reform*, 284.

164Flacius, *Bericht M. Fla. Jllyrici*, Liii v.

165Nicolaus von Amsdorff, *Ein kurtzer unterricht auff D. Georgen Maiors Antwort / das er nit unschüldig sey / wie er sich tragice rhümet* (Basel, 1552), Civ r.

166Flacius, *Bericht M. Fla. Jllyrici*, Hiii r.

ordained.[167] In addition, Flacius never pretended he was a pastor. In the end, Melanchthon also publicly rejected Major's teaching, together with other prominent theologians, and Major eventually ceased employing such speech. Major's position, which he himself later recanted, never gained much traction. Nevertheless, we see an important connection here. Only a few years after Luther's death, the teachings of original sin, free will, and now good works were under assault. The old Adam was desperately trying to work his way back into our conversion and salvation, which would be no conversion or salvation at all, because the old Adam cannot be converted and will not be saved. On the contrary, he is to be drowned, daily, as we return to our baptism in repentance—sorrow over our sin and trust in Christ for forgiveness.

In 1552 Amsdorf declared on the cover page of a pamphlet against Major, "Good works are not necessary for salvation. Good works are necessary here upon earth for a Christian life."[168] This is a succinct, biblical, orthodox, confessional Lutheran statement. Unfortunately, in opposing Major, Amsdorf eventually made the same mistake as Flacius later regarding original sin. While defending Luther's teaching, and even employing Luther's language, he employed it in a context beyond that Luther had and in a manner that could be misunderstood. In opposing Major, he "resurrected Luther's oft-repeated phrase that 'good works are detrimental to salvation,'" that is, when someone places his or her trust in them.[169] By this he did not mean truly good works, the fruits of faith, but works done in the hope of reward, to win the love of God, and not as a product of it. Amsdorf's terminology did not bring the same consequences Flacius would and thankfully this old, steadfast friend and ally of Luther and of the gospel maintained his standing within Lutheranism. While his phraseology was corrected by the Formula, he himself was not condemned by name. Rather, the

---

[167]Luka Ilić, *Theologian of Sin and Grace: The Process of Radicalization in the Theology of Matthias Flacius Illyricus* (Göttingen: Vandenhoeck & Ruprecht, 2014), 99.

[168]Amsdorff, *Ein kurtzer unterricht.*

[169]Arand, Kolb, and Nestingen, *The Lutheran Confessions*, 191–192.

Formula confessed what Amsdorf had been after with the language he adopted without condoning the language itself. In this regard, the Formula provides a wonderful reminder about the language we use in the church, especially poignant for preachers. We read:

> For, although before this controversy many pure teachers used these and similar expressions in the interpretation of the Holy Scripture, they never intended to confirm this error of the papists. Nonetheless, because later controversy over this controversy over this way expressing these ideas arose and resulted in all sorts of offensive exaggerations, it is safest to hold to St. Paul's admonition regarding the 'standard of sound teaching' (2 Tim. 1:13) as well as pure teaching itself. In this way much unnecessary quarreling can be avoided, and the church can be spared much offense.[170]

The Osiandrian Controversy over Justification

Andreas Osiander was perhaps an unexpected opponent for Flacius. Osiander had been a confessor in the fight against the Augsburg Interim. A mainstay in Nuremberg and a very influential reformer and pastor there, he had nonetheless fled the city because of his unwillingness to accept the new imperial measures. This was a courageous stand to take, no doubt, and one the Magdeburgers would have deeply respected. After he left Nuremberg, Duke Albrecht, who had been won for the reformation in part through the teaching and preaching of Osiander, created a position for him at the fledgling University of Königsberg. Safely entrenched in his new office and confident of the duke's protection, Osiander felt emboldened to speak more openly about some key differences with Luther, now dead. Most consequently, Osiander rejected Luther's emphasis on justification as a forensic act—that God, like a judge after a trial, *declares* us righteous, not guilty, for Christ's sake, of course. In so doing, he managed to do something no one else had been able to do at the time: he united the disciples of Melanchthon and Flacius, at least in disagreement with his teaching. Osiander held that the believer receives his

[170]KW, Formula of Concord, Epitome IV.36, 580.

justification through infusion rather than imputation. Justification is done into the believer rather than declared to him from outside. The internal act of the divinity of Christ in us was emphasized more than the external declaration of God for the sake of Christ the God-Man. Flacius therefore rightly identified Osiander's teaching with that of the pope, which Luther had vigorously and beyond any room for confusion rejected.

It appears that Osiander and Duke Albrecht had at first counted on Flacius' support. The duke especially assumed that Osiander's bold stand against the interims had at least earned him Flacius' silence. The duke was mistaken. Flacius later recalled, "I wanted rather to contend for the truth with my enemies in Wittenberg than against the truth with Osiander, who was then my friend."[171] He could not be silent. He was convinced that Osiander's teaching was a return to all that Luther had opposed: "That the infused love, which is also God, is our righteousness, teach the pope, Osiander and Schwenckfeld."[172] As Luther made plain on his death bed, faith was but the "beggarly hand."[173] It received what God declared. Fortunately, Osiander's misguided conception of justification never gained a true foothold within Lutheranism. While the duke continued to support him, most of the rest of Lutheranism did not. Here again, though, we see the simple, albeit profound, teaching of the *Heidelberg Disputation* and *On the Bondage of the Will* under attack. Once again, the old Adam tried to finagle his way back into our justification, to *do* something, even as a lesser partner, to *cooperate*. And the old serpent at work, slithering through small holes in that day, is still busy at work, and we do well to remain on guard. As Amsdorf insisted in the conclusion of a pamphlet against Osiander, "Therefore, the righteousness of the Christian is and can be nothing other than the righteousness of the humanity of Christ," for it was Christ, not only in His divinity,

---

[171]Olson, *Matthias Flacius and the Survival of Luther's Reform*, 287.

[172]Olson, *Matthias Flacius and the Survival of Luther's Reform*, 289. For more background, see Wilhelm Preger, *Matthias Flacius Illyricus und seine Zeit*, vol. 1 (Erlangen: T. Bläsing, 1859), 309ff.

[173]Matthias Flacius Illyricus, *Breves Summae Religionis Iesu Christi, & Antichristi* (Magdeburg: Michael Lotter, 1550), A4 r.

but also and especially in His humanity, who suffered and died for us who "are by nature yet sinners and unrighteous enemies of God." To this righteousness "we must diligently hold fast" or we have no righteousness at all.[174]

The Dispute with Schwenckfeld over Scripture

I remember once speaking to a dear relative of mine. She had begun going to a new church—not an orthodox one. She was raving about their small group Bible studies. Everybody's opinion was valid. Everyone had something to bring to the interpretation of the Bible. At one point she explained, expecting to impress me, "We just toss out a Bible verse and kick it around." I should have been more tactful and gentle, but I couldn't help myself. I simply replied, "Oh, I bet you do." By the time they were done kicking that passage there couldn't have been much life left in it. As Deutschlander observes, "As already noted, too often those who imagine that God answers prayers by blowing in their ears or whispering (apart from his Word) into their innermost beings end up pushing aside the Word and sacraments."[175] Isn't that essentially the not-so-faint echo of the first temptation in Genesis 3, after all, to have God's voice sound unmistakably like our own, to be like God, to be god? Interestingly, Schwenckfeld had been to Wittenberg twice to "interest Luther in the formation of conventicles" not all that much unlike the one attended by my relative.[176] Needless to say, he was unsuccessful. Luther was no dolt.

Flacius' literary struggle with Caspar Schwenckfeld, or as he called him, Stenkfeld, was different from the preceding controversies because it was not an inter-Lutheran battle. Schwenckfeld might not have been so vocal or open about his convictions without the

---

[174]Nicolaus von Amsdorff, *Auff Osianders Bekentnis ein Unterricht und zeugnis / Das sie Gerechtigkeit der menscheit Christi / darinnen sie entpfangen und geboren ist / allen Gleubigen Sündern geschanckt und zugerechent wird / und für ihr Person hie auff Erden nimmermehr Gerecht und heilig warden* (Magdeburg: Rödinger, 1552), Biii v.

[175]Deutschlander, *Narrow Lutheran Middle*, 75.

[176]Bente, *Historical Introductions to the Lutheran Confessions*, 355.

Reformation, but his teaching was in no way Lutheran—it would fall, if anywhere, under the umbrella of what we call the Radical Reformation, not because it was awesome, but because it sought to pull at the very roots of Christian teaching and practice. Schwenckfeld advocated a spiritual interpretation of Holy Scripture—a subjective, non-contextual, willy-nilly approach. We would all agree with the writer to the Hebrews (I am the only one on the third floor at WLC, but I think it's Paul) that the Word of God is living and active, but it lives and acts through what is written. Schwenckfeld—taking Zwingli's dichotomy farther than the Swiss reformer ever would have—sought to differentiate between letter and spirit. You had to catch the Spirit. He was not bound to what the prophets and apostles had recorded, at least not to the one simple sense. This was pure enthusiasm in Flacius' opinion. Luther would have agreed. Flacius insisted, "Spiritual exegesis [fits scripture] like a fist fits into an eye."[177] Schwenckfeld erred especially in separating God from His Means and true faith from God's revelation, emphasizing our own inner revelation.[178]

As Luther had with Erasmus, Flacius found himself defending the clarity of Scripture as well as its authority and reliability. The proper Christian hermeneutic was not a matter of inner light or mysticism. It involved an act of the mind, taken captive by Christ, shaped by faith, and employing reason in its ministerial role. You did not have to feel the Spirit. The Spirit did not work on hunches. No, Flacius insisted, the Spirit was active in and through the Word, written and faithfully preached. The Spirit and the letter were not in opposition; the Spirit worked through the letter. It was, after all, the Spirit who inspired the Scriptures, so that still today they accomplish God's purpose, which hasn't changed: the salvation of sinners, for whom Christ died and rose. One did not need to fit the Scriptures to the times. The Scriptures fit every time quite well, for they are God's timeless promise to those bound by time but created for eternity. Whereas the other controversies attacked key teachings

---

[177]Olson, *Matthias Flacius and the Survival of Luther's Reform*, 302.

[178]Matthias Flacius Illyricus, *Von fürnemlichem stücke / punct / order artikel der Schwenkfeldischen schwermerey* (Magdeburg, 1553), Ai v-Aii r. He expanded his critique in *Etliche Contradictiones . . . des Stenckfeldts daraus sein Geist leichtlich kan geprüfet warden* (Nürmnerg. 1556).

of the Reformation, Schwenckfeld attacked the very foundations, the source from which all true teaching flows. He traded one pope for many, not quite unlike the postmodernity we encounter, even in much of American Christianity. By calling into the question the clear meaning of God's revelation, Schwenckfeld called into question all that God had revealed, including the person and work of Jesus Christ. Flacius found himself debating someone who refused to use the same terms and submit to the same authorities. We know the feeling all too well. We can learn, then, from how Flacius and our fathers approached this challenge and undertook their response. As it was wont to do, the Formula said it well: "Fundamental, enduring unity in the church requires above all else a clear and binding summary and form in which a general summary of teaching is drawn together from God's Word, to which the churches that hold the true Christian religion confess their adherence."[179]

The Flacian Controversy over Original Sin

Irene Dingel summarizes the heart of the dispute over original sin thusly: "The critical difference between Strigel and the viewpoint of Flacius and also Luther lay in Strigel's failure to define conversion as a new creation, a revitalization of the spiritually dead, but rather as a reactivation of powers dormant in sinners, even before conversion—a slumbering, unconscious, but nonetheless real power." Ultimately and significantly, "[Strigel] believed this made it possible to speak of responsible decision-making by the individual."[180] Flacius reciprocated Strigel's collegial discomfort on confessional, not personal, grounds. He suspected that his coworker was a Philippist, and he was right. Strigel's later teaching amply justifies Flacius' suspicions, as Strigel eventually adopted manifestly Reformed positions on the Lord's Supper and other disputed doctrines. This raises an important issue regarding Flacius' character. While many have painted him a volatile and unbrotherly spirit, his writings hardly evidence or bear out this caricature. Diarmaid MacCulloch provides a fine

[179]KW, *Formula of Concord, Solid Declaration*, 1, 526.

[180]Dingel, "Culture of Conflict," 50.

example of the shallow and unsubstantiated stereotype of Flacius' person that is presented in much of the English historiography to date. In passing, MacCulloch essentially dismisses Flacius as "chief among these watchful, angry souls" who opposed the Interims, one of the Lutheran "ayatollahs" of that age.[181] Serious consideration of what we know for certain regarding his personal deportment and behavior, even in the midst of bitter controversy, divorced from the testimony of enemies with a vested interest in the besmirchment of his reputation, belies any charges of emotional instability or personal pettiness. In fact, his willingness to discuss (and not merely shout down) doctrinal differences, often with greater charity than his opponents, led the Illyrian, who held the upper hand in Jena and could have abused it, to accept the duke's invitation to a debate with Strigel in the first place. There is no reason to doubt that he sincerely wanted to win over his rival and restore peace to the faculty. And this was certainly Duke John Frederick's intention: the theological reconciliation of two of his university's most recognizable and respected professors. Unfortunately, the *Weimar Disputation*, begun 2 August 1560, instead tragically dashed, yes, irreparably shattered, the duke's hope for peace among his university's shining lights. Here, months after Melanchthon's death, Strigel, one of Melanchthon's few disciples at Jena, set a trap from which Flacius could not—or would not—extricate himself.

The Flacian Controversy over original sin, which the *Formula of Concord* sought to address in Article I, tellingly followed by Article II on free will, was born of this *Weimar Disputation*. The debate's chief focus was free will, but discussion eventually, and understandably, moved to original sin. Dingel notes, "The question of the free human will led directly to the topic of original sin. Comments on the free will and its capabilities presupposed a definition of original sin and its implications for the human condition."[182] While Flacius entered the debate at Weimar confident that he and Strigel could

[181]Diarmaid MacCulloch, *The Reformation: A History* (New York: Penguin Books, 2005), 349; Diarmaid MacCulloch, *The Boy King: Edward VI and the Protestant Reformation* (Berkeley: University of California Press, 2002), 170.

[182]Dingel, "Culture of Conflict," 51.

quickly reach agreement, which he earnestly sought, his career, reputation, and entire life took an unfortunate turn.[183] This happened in part because the Illyrian's defense of Luther's doctrine wasn't properly understood in the kindest possible way and under the best construction, but rather exploited by his opponents, and in part—indeed, in large part—because of his refusal to concede the dangers and misunderstandings associated with his language.

The chief sticking point of the debate developed when Strigel introduced Aristotelian language. This was in stark contrast to Flacius' hermeneutic. His monumental *Clavis Scripturae Sacrae*, or *Key to the Sacred Scriptures*, is particularly striking for its emphasis on biblically defined categories and language to the considerable exclusion of the Aristotelian.[184] Strigel endeavored to distinguish between the substance and accidents of human nature, that is, he argued that original sin was not an essential part of humanity. In Aristotelian philosophy, a substance is something that cannot be lost for a thing to be a thing, in this case, for a human to be human. Strigel was correct in asserting that original sin is not the substance of humanity, in so far as our dear Lord Jesus was truly human and yet lacked original sin. Nevertheless, in speaking of original sin as an accident, that is, something like the color of our eyes or the thickness of our hair, he failed to do justice to the depth of human depravity. Dingel explains, "Strigel correctly identified this distinction as widely-used; he was wrong in thinking it could help understand the biblical teaching on original sin and the free will. Flacius recognized correctly why that would not work, but he nonetheless decided to use this terminology which could only set the question in a false framework."[185] In other words, Flacius should have steered the discussion away from Aristotelian terminology; he should have refused to operate on the basis of philosophical and not theological language. And yet he failed to do just that. He accepted Strigel's terms and employed them intemperately. He fell into Strigel's trap. The debate proceeded as follows:

---

[183]Dingel, "Culture of Conflict," 51.

[184]Arand, Kolb, and Nestingen, *The Lutheran Confessions*, 206.

[185]Dingel, "Culture of Conflict," 52.

> Strigel pressed Flacius, "*An negas peccatum originis esse accidens?*" "Do you deny original sin is an accident?"
>
> Flacius stood with Luther: "*Luther diserte negat esse accidens.*" "Luther clearly denies it is an accident."
>
> Strigel persisted, "*Visne negare peccatum esse accidens?*" "Do you really want to deny that sin is an accident?"
>
> Flacius tragically replied, "*Quod sit substantia, dixi Scripturam et Lutherum affirmare.*" "That it is a substance, I have already stated that Scripture and Luther affirm."[186]

Thus, "fatally, Flacius followed his colleague into the swamp of joining biblical concepts and Aristotelian categories; he tried to express the biblical understanding of sin within this alien paradigm."[187] Bente writes, "Thus he fell into the pitfall which the wily Strigel had adroitly laid for him."[188] His colleagues, both in Weimar and later, pled with Flacius to see the Manichaean baggage connected with his terminology and consider the impression, false or not, that such language could create. More fatal than his choice to accept and partake in Strigel's use of Aristotelian language, however, was his unwillingness to surrender what he considered to be the language and imagery of Luther and the Bible, and more importantly, the teaching of Luther and the Bible. Throughout he would appeal to Scriptures description of sin as "flesh," of the "stony heart" of men, and other similar pictures.[189]

It is important to note that Flacius' teaching concerning original sin was more nuanced than many have presented it to be in theological and historical accounts of the debate. Flacius did distinguish between *substantia materialis* and *substantia formalis*, material substance and formal substance.[190] The material remained intact after the fall into sin, but not the formal. The material was

[186]Bente, *Historical Introductions to the Lutheran Confessions*, 337.

[187]Arand, Kolb, and Nestingen, *The Lutheran Confessions*, 206.

[188]Bente, *Historical Introductions to the Lutheran Confessions*, 336.

[189]Bente, *Historical Introductions to the Lutheran Confessions*, 337.

[190]See Matthias Flacius, *Clavis Scripturae, seu de Sermone Sacrarum Literarum, plurimas generals Regulas continens. Altera Pars.* (Basel, 1567), 479–498.

morally neutral, neither good nor evil. The formal, however, Flacius divided into two parts, a higher and a lower. Free will belonged to the higher, *substantia formalis in summon gradu*. Christman notes that in Flacius' view the higher grade "originally gave humankind its true character" and thus "was the measure by which theology judged the essence of man."[191] Christman continues, "Because [the formal substance in the highest grade] has been turned into its evil opposite in the fall into sin, it now controlled man. So technically speaking, not all of human nature was substantially originally sin, but those components that were not had been so completely subjugated to the thralldom of original sin that the distinction was now moot."[192]

Dingel writes about the controversy, "Since Strigel drew the conclusion that in fallen sinners the power to do the good and moral remained, Flacius felt challenged to emphasize the total sinfulness of the human being."[193] And that is just what Flacius did, and he did so by adopting language Luther himself had used, although without the proper sense, since Luther had never employed such language in a philosophical context where Aristotelian categories were in play. Flacius' unwillingness to allow the will any role in man's salvation, thereby diminishing the work of Christ and the complete and completed nature of his sacrifice, drove him to oppose Strigel, and yet it drove him too far in so doing, into speech that was poorly defined in the debate, and if not in Flacius' own mind, in the minds of most others. However, Flacius understood the terms in question, most comprehended them through an Aristotelian lens.

Bente explains, "The palpable mistake of Flacius was that he took the substantial terms on which he based his theory in their original and proper sense, while the Bible and Luther employ them in a figurative meaning, as the *Formula of Concord* carefully explains in its first article, which decided and settled this controversy."[194] For

---

[191]Robert J. Christman, "'*Wir sindt nichts den eytel sunde*': The Impact of Flacius' Theology of Original Sin on the German Territory of Mansfeld," in *Matija Vlačić Illirik [III]* (Labin: Grad Labin, 2012), 109.

[192]Christman, "'*Wir sindt nichts den eytel sunde*,'" 110.

[193]Dingel, "Culture of Conflict," 52.

[194]Bente, *Historical Introductions to the Lutheran Confessions*, 337.

instance, in his Genesis lectures, Luther had written "that the fall into sin had caused such a transformation of the whole person that its essential characteristics that constitute its being in the image of God are not longer present."[195] Luther had also used the metaphor of a block of stone or wood—a picture that the Formula would caution against for fear of misunderstanding—in order to describe the sinner in conversion, as well as the metaphor of the sinner as a beast of burden ridden by God or the devil. In the course of the debate, Strigel had called Luther's language on absolute necessity, especially as it appeared in *De servo arbitrio*, a "horrid way of speaking," and so Flacius felt himself obligated to defend, not only the biblical doctrine of original sin, but also the language of his mentor and theological hero.[196] Bente surmises, "In making his statement concerning the substantiality of original sin, the purpose of Flacius was to wipe out the last vestige of spiritual powers ascribed to natural man by Strigel, and to emphasize the doctrine of total corruption, which Strigel denied. His fatal blunder was that he did so in terms which were universally regarded as savoring of Manicheism."[197] Klann writes, "Unfortunately, Flacius good theological intention was soon displaced by academic pride."[198] Whether pride was at fault is hard to assess, as we cannot see Flacius' heart, and yet it was Flacius' refusal to change his language, and not his theological intention, that led to his downfall and rebuttal by the Formula. To the end he defended what he considered to be Luther's teaching and Luther's own language. He failed, however, to craft his language in accordance with the different way in with both sides were using the chief terms in the debate.

---

[195]Dingel, "Culture of Conflict," 52.

[196]Kolb, *Bound Choice*, 160–161.

[197]Bente, *Historical Introductions to the Lutheran Confessions*, 337.

[198]R. Klann, "Article I. Original Sin," in *A Contemporary Look at the Formula of Concord*, ed. Wilbert Rosin and Robert Preus (St. Louis: Concordia Publishing House, 1978), 116.

Irene Dingel, "The Culture of Conflict in the Controversies Leading to the Formula of Concord (1548–1560)," in *Lutheran Ecclesiastical Culture, 1550–1675*, ed. Robert Kolb (Leiden: Brill, 2008), 15–64.

Some have attributed Flacius' embroilment in yet another theologians' quarrel to well-night pathological obsession with doctrinal exactitude, and especially an exactitude measured according to his own opinions. Oversight of doctrine was a part of Flacius' call to Jena, however, and that should not be forgotten. The call document charged him to take care "that no one should introduce new doctrines and ceremonies, and that each pastor persevere in the religion established in the land."[199] While not obsessive, he was expected to be very attentive. Moreover, Flacius had not sought this fight. Strigel had brought it to him. Ilić faults Flacius for "not tending to unity" in such disagreements, and there is some measure of truth in that, but Flacius' conception of unity was certainly more akin to Luther's than that of the Lutheran World Federation and the progressive Lutheranism of the twentieth and twenty-first centuries. To weigh him in the scales of a Lutheranism neither he nor his opponents would have recognized is not advisable. Flacius certainly enjoyed and sought unity, but for him true unity must be unity in the truth, and especially in the chief truth, justification by grace, through faith. And that is precisely what Flacius saw under attack through any attempt to rehabilitate the image and role of the will. Christman rightly notes, "Flacius' goal was to demonstrate unequivocally that humankind in no way contributed to its own salvation."[200]

Lutheranism at this time "had been granted institutional status and had spread in many territories."[201] This did bode well for the survival of Lutheran institutions. Flacius was not concerned with institutional survival, however. It was the Wittenbergers who fretted for the future of their university and thus compromised. One will struggle in vain in the Book of Concord to find a primary, sustained, or even passing concern for the institutional status of the Lutheran Church, however. Lutheranism from its beginning has been about doctrine (doctrine was unquestionably unitary for Luther), a proclamation, a dialectic of law and gospel. For

[199]Ilić, *Theologian of Sin and Grace*, 135.

[200]Christman, "'*Wir sindt nichts den eytel sunde*,'" 110.

[201]Ilić, *Theologian of Sin and Grace*, 142.

better or for worse Luther drew no blueprint for the institutional status of Lutheranism, although the visitations were a step in that direction. What Flacius was obsessed with was the survival of God's Word and Luther's teaching, the preservation of Christ's gospel in Word and Sacrament in truth and purity. Flacius was "adamant about holding on to his theological positions by not showing any willingness to rethink or modify them," but his motivation for acting as he did was rooted in more than a personality defect.[202] His adamancy sprang from his bondage to the Scriptures. Where Flacius was convinced that God spoke, there Flacius was unwilling to waver, even an inch, no matter the personal and professional cost. Such stubbornness has no doubt marked both church fathers and heretics throughout the history of Christianity—serving one well and the other poorly in the eyes of the orthodox. Flacius' stubbornness drove him into both ditches, so to speak, so that he was both vindicated and condemned by the Formula of Concord, so that he both defended confessional Lutheran doctrine and clouded it, the former with respect to his teaching on adiaphora and the latter his position on original sin.

It is important to understand, too, that Flacius and the Gnesio-Lutherans who labored in the Synergistic Controversy, including Amsdorf, who had his own intemperate words carefully repudiated in the Formula, did not reject the obligation of new obedience. Some might, and indeed have, mistakenly drawn such a conclusion. Robert Kolb refutes such a notion:

> Throughout their writings the Gnesio-Lutheran critics of Strigel and Pfeffinger insisted on the obligations of new obedience. They strove to make clear to their hearers and readers that God had created human beings to function responsibly according to his divine definition of what it means to be human. Like Luther, when engaged in the defense of God's total responsibility for all things, they expressed his sovereign control of his creation with an emphasis on the bondage of the will. That did not mean that they wished to sacrifice their avowal of the integrity of the human creature and of the active nature of the

[202]Ilić, *Theologian of Sin and Grace*, 157.

> human will in the midst of its captivity to Satan. They sought to proclaim both law and gospel and hold them in tension.[203]

Kolb's description of the teaching of Nicolaus Gallus, a fellow Magdeburg confessor with Flacius and Amsdorf, and likely the author of the Magdeburg Confession, a work worthy of more contemporary study and research, helps clarify the teaching of the Gnesio-Lutherans on sanctification and new obedience:

> On the basis of *De servo arbitrio*, Nikolaus Gallus rejected the idea that the free will apart from God's aid has any power to repent and practice the Christian life, even as he acknowledged the necessity of this life of repentance and obedience. Such a recognition permeated the preaching and teaching of Gallus and his contemporaries. They had indeed grasped that God repeats and renews the baptismal death and resurrection he had given sinners throughout life because, for some mysterious and hidden reason, believers still must struggle against their own sinfulness. . . . Like Luther, they believed that God had bound his human creatures to trust and the obedience it produces in his shaping of their humanity. They proclaimed Christ's liberation from the bondage to sin and Satan into which these creatures had fallen. They sought to cultivate a life of love, that is, true human freedom, by binding their hearers once again to God's promises in Christ.[204]

Flacius certainly employed language that lent itself to misunderstanding, and he spoke in ways that flouted the conventional, Aristotelian use of terms employed for centuries, but Flacius was no heretic, although he certainly failed the test according to the famous Augustinian maxim, "*Errare possum, hereticus esse nolo*," that is, "I might err, but I will not be a heretic." Flacius certainly persisted in his language after others, even allies, raised concerns about it, in language condemned later by the Formula of Concord—and yet language he held to be Scripture's and Luther's own—but in what he sought to defend in the debate over original sin, he endeavored to

---

[203]Kolb, *Bound Choice*, 165.

[204]Kolb, *Bound Choice*, 166.

be no false teacher. A lifelong experience with persecution, doctrinal controversy, and spiritual and militaristic assaults upon Luther's Reformation had marked and shaped him, had made him desperate to preserve the truth of Scripture and the gospel of Jesus Christ. He indeed held to Luther's words, but the Formula better grasped and explicated their sense. Flacius' chief fault rested in his linguistic obstinacy, not in his desire to defend the teaching of the Scriptures and his spiritual father, Martin Luther. If he was anything, Matthias Flacius Illyricus was consistent. He who had called others to bear the cross and stand firm in their confession of the Word of God and Luther's teaching stood firm in his convictions. After another conflict with the duke, this time concerning the freedom of the church from the state, he was forced to flee and lost his position as a professor.[205] Sadly, after a long succession of exiles, he died an isolated, wandering man in Frankfurt am Main in 1575. Even more sadly, as a result of his confession and his controversial nature, he was denied a Christian burial.[206] The cross marked even his death, as he likely long expected it would, if not his grave.

In many ways the Formula was a vindication of Gnesio-Lutheran concerns and emphases, while a critique of their language and temperament. One thing the Formula most certainly wasn't was Melanchthonian or Philippist in theological orientation, although it was Melanchthonian in structure, tone, and clarity. It must be remembered that almost all of those involved in the controversies that led to the Formula and those that crafted the Formula were students of Melanchthon. Even as we might bemoan the damage Melanchthon's later wavering, moderating, and revising did to Lutheranism, we must acknowledge Lutheranism's immense debt to the Praeceptor as well. He trained his students well, so well indeed, that they stood on guard even against his own deviations and molded a clear, concise, and lasting Formula, which merged the best of his own theology and

---

[205]Oliver Olson, "Matthias Flacius (1520–1575)," in *The Reformation Theologians: An Introduction to the Early Modern Period*, ed. Carter Lindberg (Oxford: Blackwell, 2002), 87.

[206]Oliver Olson, "Matthias Flacius (1520–1575)," 88.

temperament with Luther's. Not only was Flacius a "Schüler Luthers und Melanchthons," but so were the Concordists as well.[207]

The Concordists repudiated Flacius' language concerning original sin without naming him specifically. Rather, they referred to "Manichaean error."[208] They "argued that Flacius's view of original sin would twist and pervert the doctrines of creation, redemption, sanctification, and the resurrection of the flesh, for in each case it would ascribe false characteristics to the actions of God and to the created nature of his human creature."[209] After explaining the proper sense in which Luther's use of the terms "nature-sin," "person-sin," or "essential sin," should be understood, the Formula did speak of original sin as "embedded in the human being's nature, substance, and essence."[210] It is not human nature or substance, but embedded in it, which respected Flacius' sensitivities even as it rejected his language. "The Concordists were deeply concerned that the people of God might get the impression that God was responsible in any way for sin."[211] In this manner, they shared Melanchthon's fear, and correctly so, without, however, adopting Melanchthon's emphasis on human responsibility and the three causes of conversion, which the Praeceptor had intended as a corrective. They left no doubt that original sin is a deep corruption of the human nature and no slight infirmity or minor defect. "The Formula insisted on the totality of this corruption of human creatures through sin but also insisted that the fallen sinner remains truly a creation of God, a creature whom God redeems, sanctifies, and raises from the dead as his own human child."[212] The Concordists affirmed the passivity of the human will in conversion while cautioning against misunderstanding Luther's description of the will as "*pure passive*" in a manner that might give

---

207 Dingel, "Flacius als Schüler," 77–93.

208 KW, *Formula of Concord, Epitome* I.9, 490.

209 Arand, Kolb, and Nestingen, *The Lutheran Confessions*, 209.

210 KW, *Formula of Concord, Epitome* I.20, 490; KW, *Formula of Concord, Epitome* I.21, 490.

211 Arand, Kolb, and Nestingen, *The Lutheran Confessions*, 209.

212 Arand, Kolb, and Nestingen, *The Lutheran Confessions*, 210.

the impression that the converted functioned in no way psychologically in the process. The Formula counsels in Article II:

> [It must be understood] insofar as God's Spirit takes hold of the human will through the Word that is heard or through the use of the holy sacraments and effects new birth and conversion. For when the Holy Spirit has effected and accomplished new birth and conversion and has altered and renewed the human will solely through this divine power and activity, then the new human will is an instrument and tool of God the Holy Spirit, in that the will not only accepts grace but also cooperates with the Holy Spirit in the works that proceed from it.[213]

Notice, however, that the will is an instrument, not a cause, in conversion. God alone, acting through the Means of Grace, is the cause. The Concordists insist in Article II: "As little as a corpse can make itself alive for bodily, earthly life, so little can people who through sin are spiritually dead raise themselves up to spiritual life."[214] In the end, the Concordists accomplished what Flacius could not. They stepped back, considered the concerns of all the parties involved—what they were trying to defend from the truth of God—and pondered, not what language could possibly be used, but rather what language best served the biblical concepts and images involved. In this way, the controversy was settled for roughly two-thirds of Lutheranism in Germany and a valuable theological treasure was bequeathed to subsequent generations, in Germany, here in America, and throughout the world.

---

[213]KW, *Formula of Concord, Epitome* II.18, 494.

[214]KW, *Formula of Concord, Epitome* II.3, 492.

Lessons from the "Culture of Conflict"

The Significance of Original Sin for Pastoral Care and Preaching

Steven D. Paulson has put it brutally beautifully when he writes, "Inner-blind and outer-dead people are a very poor demographic for making worship work."[215] The gospel isn't a "would ya like," but a "thus saith the Lord." God promises. Christians believe, because God promises. The gospel is unlike anything in this world. It is trustworthy, in every instance. It gives what it says, always. It does as if already done—indeed, it is as good as done before the believer even knows it is doing. We therefore do not woo the dead. God raises them through us, through His Means for which we merely serve as unimpressive and most unworthy feet, hands, and mouths. We live in a fallen world and deal with fallen people. We are fallen people in a fallen world. This is not an aspect of our existence. This is our existence. It is into this mess and mire that the Christ comes.

Flacius was intemperate in his language and stubborn in his persistence in that language, but his chief concern—the peculiar truth of the Bible and Luther's proper emphasis of it—remains pertinent. First, we are reminded of the value of humility and a willingness to admit, not only when we have spoken incorrectly, but also when we have spoken carelessly. The preacher must strive not only to speak in

---

[215]Steven D. Paulson, "What Is Essential in Lutheran Worship," *Word & World* 26, nr. 1 (Spring 2006): 154.

such a way that he can be understood properly but also in such a way that he cannot be easily misunderstood. Walther advises, "Another point you should bear in mind when writing your sermons is not to say anything that might be misunderstood."[216]

Furthermore, we learn from the Flacian Controversy that as pastors we must take into account, acknowledge, appreciate, and articulate the lostness, the condemnedness, the fallenness, the depravity of the human condition and nature. It is meaningful that Article II and Article XVIII of the Augustana alike condemn and reject the Pelagians, Augustine's vexing and formidable foes. This is no coincidence. Moreover, Article II explicitly asserts that those who admit works into justification diminish the glory of Christ's merits and benefits. This is crucial. How many aren't offended at the notion that Jesus, and thus His Bride, do not primarily exist in order to make good people? That is the truth, though. As a pastor, I was not very concerned at all with my people's sins. I was much more concerned with their repentance, which of course embraces and is realized only through faith. I didn't want to make my people good people. I wanted to make them the most despicable and wretched scoundrels. That is, I wanted to convince them that they were such. Deutschlander warns, "It is surprising sometimes to find that people who are no longer coarse sinners have become refined Pharisees"—no battle is won in that, the field has merely shifted.[217] The *Apology* explains, "The benefits of Christ cannot be recognized unless we understand our evil."[218] And this has consequences for preaching. People must know who they are without Christ. "Therefore our preachers have diligently taught about these matters," the Apology states. People simply and literally have no chance in hell of being good people until they admit they are bad people—people who have lost the image of God. And even then, they cannot become good people through any new morality. They can become good people only through Christ and His Word, through Jesus' resurrection from the

---

216 C. F. W. Walther, *Law and Gospel: How to Read and Apply the Bible*, trans. Christian C. Tiews (St. Louis: Concordia Publishing House, 2010), 62.

217 Deutschlander, *Narrow Lutheran Middle*, 43.

218 KW, *Apology of the Augsburg Confession* II.50, 120.

dead, which is our reconciliation and justification—a reconciliation and justification *for sinners*. Any other approach robs Christ of His proper glory. Article IV must precede Article VI, and Article VI can come only through Article V. There is no other way that accords with the Scriptures and Christ's honor. Will my people sin less? I hope so. Will my people then do some good works? How can they not, for Christ dwells in them? Will my people, though, then be better people, in civic righteousness, than Joe Unbeliever? Maybe, maybe not, because sometimes Joe Unbeliever can be a swell guy. What's the solution when my people fail to be the good people the world and many misguided people expect me to make them? It's time to make them lousy people again. It's time to convict them of their sin. And then it's time, not to tell them to lift themselves up by their bootstraps, not to stage an intervention, not to give them a Dr. Phil talking-to, but to send Christ down into the gutter with them again, to speak Absolution, through which Christ, and not the sinner, does the lifting and cleansing.

Pastors, you have a congregation of saints, but they remain sinners, just like you. And sinners sin. Sometimes they sin marvelously—whoppers, dandies, front page sort of sins. Don't let them see you act shocked when they confess their sins. Don't let them think for a moment that they shouldn't come to you with those sins. Don't give the impression that they are less Christian when they have come to you to confess them—not to be convicted, for God has already worked that, but to be absolved—for in seeking absolution they are doing the most Christian thing of all, something only the Spirit can prompt. Rather, be concerned about the hundreds who consider their sins too lightly to address them, too frivolous for God to give much of a whoop, who are just glad to avoid the whoppers, the dandies, the "front page" sort of sins. This too is natural, but obviously not edifying or salutary. John Meyer writes, "Natural man likes to think of God as one who will overlook our shortcomings."[219] Even Christian pastors fall into this trap, as you know all too well from the iniquity of your own hearts and minds. We wouldn't get

---

[219]John Meyer, *Studies in the Augsburg Confession* (Milwaukee: Northwestern Publishing House, 1995), 33.

so angry if it weren't for the stress. We wouldn't yell at our spouses or children if we could stick up for ourselves with anyone else. We wouldn't, we wouldn't, we wouldn't . . . We expect God to overlook our transgressions but somehow notice and praise and amply reward the insignificant and trifling menstrual rags we deem "good" works. We want to be on the front page, not for our depravity, but for our righteousness—emphasis on the "our." Luther's warning from the Smalcald Articles comes to mind: "This inherited sin has caused such a deep, evil corruption of nature that reason does not comprehend it; rather, it must be believed on the basis of the revelation in the Scriptures."[220] Thankfully, those Scriptures remind us what is front page news in heaven: one sinner who repents.

We need to be the sinner. Our people need to be the sinner. Why? Because sinners sin and pastors forgive sinners (and pastors forgive sinners who are pastors)—repentant sinners—because pastors serve as the ambassadors of Christ, who forgave us our sins when were yet His enemies, when we were but a twinkle in our parents' eyes. And no, I'm not asking you to excuse your peoples' sins. I'm not asking you to downplay their sins at all. I am simply asking you to forgive them for what they are—fruits of original sin, the handiwork of the sinful nature. Get wet in such moments. Drown the sinful nature again through the third Sacrament. Give the devil a kick in his pants, because the devil can use guilt just as God can—He can drive the sorrowful sinner to despair—but the devil cannot touch guilt when God has wiped it away, blotted it out, cast it far as the east is from the west. Lazarus wasn't ashamed to admit how dead he was. He wasn't embarrassed of his linen cloths. Much to the contrary, his deadness and those cloths testified to the love of Christ, just what a marvelous, miraculous, mind-boggling thing Jesus had done, unasked and unearned, but certainly not uneventful or unworthy of unending praise.

Ultimately, the church's task is not simply or chiefly transformative, but baptismal, and thankfully so. The Spirit's primary task is not to transform sinners in the way that too many churches advertise, but to make them new. Yes, a transformation takes place. Paul writes

---

[220]KW, *Smalcald Articles* III.1.3, 311.

in Romans 12:2, with the mercies of God pressed upon us in the preceding verse, and more importantly, by the entire letter to that point, "*Do not be conformed to this world, but be transformed by the renewal of your mind, that by testing you may discern what is the will of God, what is good and acceptable and perfect.*" This transformation, however, is not the sort measured in tallies of sins and works—works, as we've covered, will follow, but this is not the chief task of the church and it is the fruit of the gospel, not the gospel. The Spirit is not in this for a quick buck. He does not come in and flip a house. No, He renews it and makes it His own temple, His own eternal dwelling place. This is not a matter of some paint and new floors. The Holy Spirit kills and makes alive, drowns and raises. Transformation, as we understand it, is often measured in law. Baptism is measured in crosses, Christ's cross traced upon our head and our heart and the crosses we bear for Him. As Melanchthon was tempted and moved to turn his focus from the gospel to the law, from election to obedience, on account of the Saxon Visitation, so we can be tempted to lose focus on account of the state of our parishes and society in general. Does your church seem dead? Rejoice. Jesus loves to raise dead things. Does your Christian walk seem limp and lame? Take heart, those are the horses our Lord chooses to harness. We are who we are, but Jesus is who He is, and we are now who we are in Jesus, and in that we have certainty, consolation, and real hope.

Adiaphora and the Connection between Doctrine and Practice[221]

Disputes over worship practices, as we have seen, have a long history in Lutheranism. From early on they can be found in the American setting, especially as Lutherans wrestled with just how their rather un-American faith would find a home within American culture—if that were even possible. Nelson recalls regarding the temptation to revivalism:

---

[221]Much of what follows in this section has been reproduced or adapted from Wade R. Johnston, "Article X of the Formula of Concord and Lutheranism Today," *Lutheran Synod Quarterly* 50, nr. 1 (March 2010): 67–94.

> In addition to the language difficulties there was the controversial issue of revivalism. When, in the wake of the revolutionary war and the subsequent westward movements, individuals and groups frequently became detached from their churches, revivalism offered a means to renew and reawaken spiritual life. Protracted meetings and enthusiastic and emotional outbursts were often employed in attempting renewal. Some Lutherans were not immune to such methods and considered them spiritually vitalizing. In fact, sometimes Lutherans rivaled the Methodists, Baptists, and Finneyites in employing the techniques of the revivalistic system.[222]

New practices, or new measures, were not indifferent, however, as much as those adopting them may have thought. They came with baggage. The Lutherans who adopted revivalistic methods soon began to walk, talk, and believe like the American Protestants they mimicked. Nelson notes:

> A dichotomy appeared between "head" and "heart" Christians . . . Where revivalistic techniques were employed consistently, the central doctrine of justification by faith in Christ was endangered and the theological complexion often became Arminian. The denial of original sin followed and the sinner was granted the ability to cooperate with God in the act of justification. Luther's catechism fell into disuse.[223]

Wentz' explains the tensions that developed between the Pennsylvania Ministerium and its more revivalistic neighbors who nonetheless still claimed the title "Lutheran," and, for all accounts and purposes, likely with very sincere convictions that they were forwarding the cause of Lutheranism. He writes:

> The predominating influences in the [Pennsylvania] Ministerium were German, and they harbored a strong aversion to the remnant of revivalism and Puritanism that still lingered in some parts of the

[222]Clifford E. Nelson, *The Lutherans in North America* (Philadelphia: Fortress Press, 1975), 215.

[223]Nelson, *Lutherans in North America*, 216.

> General Synod. The Ministerium was in more direct touch with the Lutheran reaction in Germany and its inspiring literature, made more constant use of Luther's Catechism and German hymns, and received a larger number of German pastors. All this deepened the Lutheran convictions of the Ministerium beyond those of other synods.[224]

We do well to note the significant mooring role that worship methods, styles, customs, etc. played in the doctrinal leanings of the more conservative Pennsylvania Ministerium.[225] The catholic principle, so often tested, once again proved correct: *lex orandi, lex credendi*. This was so, however, because the *lex credendi* conversely determined the *lex orandi*. The experience of the Pennsylvania Ministerium also provides a strong reinforcement of the importance of continued publication of sound, orthodox, carefully vetted literature, both works of the past and those produced in our own day, for the preservation of our theological and liturgical vitality. Much mischief can be started on the pastor's bookshelf, in the parish's library, and on the musician's stand. We do well to be attentive to what might end up there and, in love, to encourage one another in using what is most faithful and consistent with the Scriptures and our Confessions.

Flacius and Article X of the Formula remind us of the vice versa relationship of the catholic principle. Both the *orandi* and the *credendi* can rightly claim first place in the formula. In fact, a confessional and ancient/historical church like the Evangelical Lutheran Church will insist on such a reciprocal relationship. Article X of the Formula has no use for "we've always done it that way," "whatever works," "it's what the people like," "must," "should," "have to," or "who cares." Rather, the confessors looked to the one fountain that truly issues "good order," "Christian discipline," and "evangelical propriety," that is, the Word of God, and they then sought to practice, with

---

[224]Abdel Ross Wentz, *A Basic History of Lutheranism in America* (Philadelphia: Muhlenberg Press, 1955), 155.

[225]Several synods influenced by revivalism and the Americanization include the following: the Hartwick Synod, the Melanchthon Synod, and the Franckean Synod. The admission of the latter to the General Synod in 1861 led to that body's eventual decline, including the withdrawal of the Pennsylvania Ministerium.

an eye toward their received tradition, but without being handcuffed by it, that which best reflected such a relationship between doctrine and practice, practice and doctrine.

Armand Boehme drives home this point:

> For early Lutherans, *lex credendi* had precedence over *lex orandi*. They clearly saw the "law of believing founds the law of worshipping." Central to faith and belief is the doctrine of justification, the article by which the church stands or falls. Therefore the Lutheran Confessions emphasize the fact that "worship is thoroughly grounded in the doctrine of justification and justification becomes the touchstone for liturgical change and adaptation." The Lutheran Confessions note that the term *liturgy* is not seen as a work or action of the people; rather *liturgy* has to do with God's working through the office of the holy ministry to grant his grace to sinners. Thus the Confessions' emphasis is on justification in the divine liturgy, not on the sanctified work of the people in response to God's justifying grace.[226]

He continues, contrasting the approach of Anglicans and Lutherans, two of the great ancient/historical Protestant traditions:

> Thus Anglicans and Lutherans view tradition differently. For Anglicans tradition (*lex orandi*) has near (if not equal) authority with Holy Scripture (*lex credendi*). Furthermore, tradition is something that continues to unfold as the Spirit gives insight. For Lutherans good traditions are respected, but all tradition is subordinate to Holy Scripture. In fact, if tradition is contrary to Scripture it must be rejected, and all the more so if the tradition conflicts with the doctrine of justification.[227]

This is nothing other than an articulation of Article X, a practice rooted in doctrine, respectful of tradition, but captive to the Word of God, keenly aware that only the gospel can do the work of the gospel,

---

[226]Armand Boehme, "'But We've Always Done It That Way': Wittenberg and Canterbury on Tradition," *Logia: A Journal of Lutheran Theology* XII, nr. 4 (Reformation 2003): 12–13.

[227]Boehme, "But We've Always," 13.

and yet also cognizant of the influence practice can have, intentionally or unintentionally, upon the doctrinal convictions of the laity.[228]

We are often in our circles keenly aware of the danger of Romanizing, of the danger of turning to tradition and ceremony to do what only the Means of Grace can do, of shrouding what bears God's promise in the invention, albeit ancient, of men. This is a good vigilance. Smells and bells have more than once been the refuge of those who have abandoned the shelter of God's inspired Word. We don't fight on one front, however. We should be just as wary of the other ditch, too, of those who would turn to the practices of those whose roots rest in the confession and methodology of men and women who deemed Luther's Reformation incomplete and the Means of Grace ineffectual, or not effective enough, albeit while espousing a seemingly high view of the Scriptures, which has lured many to see kinship where there is in fact is little to none.[229] Luther did insist in a passage often quoted from a work not often enough read, his *Confession concerning Christ's* Supper, "Sooner than have mere wine with the fanatics, I would agree with the pope that there is only blood."[230] Tossing out tradition is no special virtue and innovation is a byword, not a boast, in the Confessions. We must always remember that evangelism springs from the God-given εὐαγγέλιον, the Good News of Jesus Christ.[231] The gospel doesn't need help. The unbeliever has no free will to woo. The old Adam has no redeemable

---

[228]Why and how someone does something in the realm of adiaphora, and not the fact that someone does it, makes a Lutheran Romanizing. The fact that the church always did something isn't necessarily a reason to do it again. In fact, it was the reintroduction of ceremonies that led to the Adiaphoristic Controversy. The fact that you have catechized your members and it helps them appropriate the gospel and honor God, however, may be a reason to reintroduce such things.

[229]Indeed, enthusiast is often an apt term in this respect.

[230]LW 37:317.

[231]Those from the Church Growth Movement camp who have harped on addressing "felt needs" as a top priority (e.g., *The Purpose Driven Church* by Rick Warren), must be reminded that the last "felt need" the sinful nature (and they are often talking about the "felt needs" of the unchurched, precisely the people who have only the sinful nature to guide their perception of what they

desire to which we can appeal. In this regard, Nietzsche was right again, although unintentionally so. He wrote:

> This is the same logic as: "if thine eye offend thee, pluck it out." In the particular case in which that dangerous "innocent from the country," the founder of Christianity, recommended this practice to his disciples, the case of sexual excitation, the consequence is, unfortunately, not only the loss of an organ but the *emasculation* of a man's character. And the same applies to the moralist's madness that demands, instead of the restraining of the passions, their extirpation. Its conclusion is always: only the castrated man is a good man.[232]

The desires of the old man must be snuffed out. They certainly must not be appealed to, surveyed, or flamed. The Formula is clear: "Likewise, we believe, teach, and confess that the unregenerate human will is not only turned away from God but has also become God's enemy, that it has only the desire and will to do evil and whatever is opposed to God."[233] No matter how many times the sinful man or woman sings a chorus about his or her love for God, he or she has none, and he or she will gain none through inane repetition. The gospel must be proclaimed, set front and center, unwrapped, not carefully and marketably packaged. The visitor's hope rests, not in the personality of the pastor, the melody of the hymns, the beauty of the sanctuary, or the temperature of the coffee, but in Christ who comes, as He did on Christmas, wrapped in swaddling clothes, be they water, the pastor's ugly mug, bread, or wine. "God the Holy Spirit does not effect conversion without means, but he uses preaching and the hearing of God's Word to accomplish it. . . . And it is Gods will that people hear his Word and not plug their ears."[234] As much as we want to clean out the wax, their fingers are the problem, and only the

---

need) will recognize or acknowledge is the gospel in Word and Sacrament—the foundation of the Lutheran worship service.

[232]Friedrich Nietzsche, *The Will to Power*, trans. Walter Kaufmann and R. J. Hollingdale (New York: Vintage Books, 1967), Book II. 383, 207.

[233]KW, Formula of Concord, Epitome II.3, 492.

[234]KW, Formula of Concord, Solid Declaration II.4, 492.

Spirit can pry them from free.[235] And wonderful things happen when we trust the promise and despair of our gimmicks or vain hopes of helping God's Word out: "When one is able to trust God by means of a word one speaks very differently to him—in the way a husband and wife speak to one another as opposed to the way an advertisement addresses an unknown client."[236]

Separating the two, methods and Means, doctrine and practice, essentially is to adopt a Jesuitical approach ("the end justifies the means"). This is fundamentally un-Lutheran and, more importantly, unscriptural. When the Formula says, "Moreover, we must not include among the truly free adiaphora or indifferent matters ceremonies that give the appearance or (in order to avoid persecution) are designed to give the impression that our religion does not differ greatly from the papist religion or that their religion were not completely contrary to ours," "papist" could well be changed to "Baptist," "Presbyterian," "Methodist," or any other Protestant sect (even those unwilling to identify themselves in such a way, let alone put such an identity on a sign).[237] We do well to ask ourselves, should a heterodox Christian walk into our midst, would he be aware of any differences between our confession and his, the orientation of our divine service and the orientation of his worship? Kurt Marquardt cuts to the heart with a quotation from Luther:

> If now I seek the forgiveness of sins, I dare not run to the cross, for I will not find it given there. Nor must I hold to the suffering of Christ, as Dr. Karlstadt trifles, in knowledge or remembrance, for I will not find it there either. But I will find in the Sacrament or gospel the Word which distributes, presents, offers, and gives to me that forgiveness which was won on the cross.[238]

---

[235]Just how contrary to our natural and surely well-intentioned thinking may well be demonstrated by an attempt from the floor to nuance this assertion, to allow at least some cleaning of wax.

[236]Paulson, *Lutheran Theology*, 55.

[237]KW, Formula of Concord, Solid Declaration X.5, 636

[238]Kurt Marquardt, "'Church Growth' as Mission Paradigm: A Confessional Lutheran Assessment," in *Church and Ministry Today: Three Confessional Lutheran Essays* (St. Louis: Luther Academy, 2001), 58.

His own words then cast even more light:

> In the face of the lunacies now masquerading as worship, one can only admire the wit of the woman who thought it was high time for the church "to stop trying to entertain the goats and get back to feeding the sheep" It was, one must remember, the devil who invented "entertainment evangelism" and tempted the Lord with it (Matthew 4:5, 6).[239]

In God's service, God's Word does things. The sermon does things. God does things through the pastor, not by the pastor's power, but His own. Yes, the pastor could refuse to speak, but God would not be daunted. The stones would cry out, or even better, the congregation would sing some solid Lutheran hymns. One of the most frustrating inanities spoken in our circles involves the false conception that some hymns or services are too German, they are too unemotional, they are head-heavy but heart-light. People need *practical* theology, we are sometimes told. And yet there is no practical theology without *theology.* And the Lutheran Church has always confessed that theology is a *habitus practicus*. Lutheranism has a rich history of melding the devotional and the didactic, in its sermons, its services, and its songs. Carl Schalk drives this point home:

> Such a view incorrectly implies that proclamatory hymns are merely teaching efforts, at best, or rhymed dogma, at worst. It forgets that the proclamation of the gospel is directed not only to the world as a message of hope and salvation, and to God as the community of faith pleads the good news of the gospel before the Father—just as the Son pleads for us before him—and praised him for it, but to the Christian community itself as it confesses and celebrates the faith.[240]

John Donne was not a confessor of the Evangelical Lutheran Church (he was an Anglican convert from Roman Catholicism), but

---

239Kurt Marquardt, "'Church Growth' as Mission Paradigm," 135.

240Carl F. Schalk, "Hymnody and the Proclamation of the Gospel," in *Not Unto Us: A Celebration of the Ministry of Kurt J. Eggert* (Milwaukee: Northwestern Publishing House, 2001), 138.

he was a man with common sense, something, as the saying goes, that is not so common nowadays. He wrote, "No man is an island, entire of itself." The Evangelical Lutheran Church is a church of individual believers, as our scriptural distinction between invisible and visible church, or Church within the church, shows.[241] With this in mind, however, it is important to recognize that in their conviction that "*Dissonantia ieiunii non dissolvit consonantiam fidei*" the formulators of Article X are not advocating a reckless smorgasbord of worship practices. Moreover, when the confessions recognize that different churches can have different practices, it is useful to remember that they were often thinking, not of individual congregations, as in our American voters-assembly context, but of territorial churches. Brothers and sisters were bound together in Christian love beyond the doors of their individual building. There is real value in an evangelical conformity in practice, after all. That is why we've had *The Lutheran Hymnal*, *Christian Worship*, *Evangelical Lutheran Hymnary*, and similar hymnals. It is hard for a pastor who has had time enough at his parish to put all his books on his shelves to doubt that questions will arise in the mind of Joe Pewsitter when, as he travels from WELS church to WELS church, or ELS church to ELS church, or WELS church to ELS church and vice versa, he observes a massive chasm in worship forms between parishes (and not mere subtle differences). These questions, if not answered with careful instruction and charitable patience, will inevitably lead to doubt and a loss of certainty in other areas of the Faith. Here too Article X's concern for the weak brother is imperative. The individual church and Christian must always have a concern for the benefit of the brotherhood of the faithful as a whole.

Tiefel quotes Walther:

> We refuse to be guided by those who are offended by our church customs. We adhere to them all the more firmly when someone wants to cause us to have a guilty conscience on account of them. . . . It is truly distressing that many of our fellow Christians find the differences between Lutheranism and papism in outward things. It is a

[241]KW, Formula of Concord, Solid Declaration X.19, 639.

pity and dreadful cowardice when one sacrifices the good and ancient customs to please the deluded American sects, lest they accuse us of being papistic.

Indeed! Am I to be afraid of a Methodist, who perverts the saving Word, or be ashamed in the matter of my good cause, and not rather rejoice that the sects can tell by our ceremonies that I do not belong to them?

We are not insisting that there be unity in perception or feelings or of taste among all believing Christians, neither dare anyone demand that all be minded as he. Nevertheless it remains true that the Lutheran liturgy distinguishes Lutheran worship from the worship of other churches to such an extent that the latter look like lecture halls in which the hearers are merely addressed or instructed, while our churches are in truth houses of prayer in which the Christians serve God publicly before the world.[242]

---

[242]James P. Tiefel, "The Formation and Flow of Worship Attitudes in the Wisconsin Evangelical Lutheran Synod," in *Not Unto Us: A Celebration of the Ministry of Kurt J. Eggert* (Milwaukee: Northwestern Publishing House, 2001), 149–150. The preceding paragraph from Walther's essay is also worth attention: "We know and firmly hold that the character, the soul of Lutheranism, is not found in outward observances but in the pure doctrine. If a congregation had the most beautiful ceremonies in the very best order, but did not have the pure doctrine, it would be anything but Lutheran. We have from the beginning spoken earnestly of good ceremonies, not as though the important thing were outward forms, but rather to make use of our liberty in these things. For true Lutherans know that although one does not have to have these things (because there is no divine command to have them), one may nevertheless have them because good ceremonies are lovely and beautiful and are not forbidden in the Word of God. Therefore the Lutheran church has not abolished 'outward ornaments, candles, altar cloths, statues and similar ornaments,' [AP XXIV] but has left them free. The sects proceeded differently because they did not know how to distinguish between what is commanded, forbidden, and left free in the Word of God. We remind only of the mad actions of Carlstadt and of his adherents and followers in Germany and in Switzerland. We on our part have retained the ceremonies and church ornaments in order to prove by our actions that we have a correct understanding of Christian liberty, and know how to conduct ourselves in things which are neither commanded nor forbidden by God." C. F. W. Walther, "The True Visible Church and the Form of a Christian Congregation," in *Essays for the Church* (St. Louis: Concordia Publishing House, 1992), 193–194.

Walther doesn't stop there, lest we miss his point:

> The objection: "What would be the use of uniformity of ceremonies?" was answered with the counter question, "What is the use of a flag on the battlefield?" Even though a soldier cannot defeat the enemy with it, he nevertheless sees by the flag where he belongs. We ought not to refuse to walk in the footsteps of our fathers. They were so far removed from being ashamed of the good ceremonies that they publicly confess in the passage quoted: "It is not true that we do away with all such external ornaments."[243]

It is perhaps beneficial to briefly pause and remember again at this point that the Synodical Conference was a fellowship of Lutherans who also confronted worship controversies among Lutherans, some not so different than those we witness today. Times change, people not so much. They want what they want, and what they want is not what God knows we need.

Article X, if hastily read, and with preconceived, modern, American notions, might seem to bespeak a rugged individualism in church practices. The Formula, however, was not written in a vacuum, and it was not unaware of what came before it. As the Nicene and Athanasian creeds built upon the Apostles', the Formula, and Flacius, and the other Gnesio-Lutherans who objected to the liturgical regulations of the Interims, built upon the previous Lutheran Confessions. Indeed, perhaps no one, unintentional loner that he became through later isolation on account of the controversy over original sin, appealed more to Augsburg and its Confessions than Flacius. In no way would the Gnesio-Lutherans or the Formula have repudiated Apology XXIV:

> At the outset it is again necessary, by way of preface, to point out that we do not abolish the Mass but religiously retain and defend it. Among us the Mass is celebrated every Lord's day and on other festivals, when the sacrament is made available to those who wish to partake of it, after they have been examined and absolved. We also keep

[243]Walther, "The True Visible Church," 193–4. See the preceding footnote for further context.

traditional liturgical forms, such as the order of readings, prayers, vestments, and other similar things.[244]

The Lutheran Church is not an ahistorical church disconnected from those who have gone before her, but rather one rooted in the past and deeply aware of her indebtedness to the earlier confessors who have passed down to her the pure doctrine she holds so dear, and, at her best, constantly strives in whatever way possible to hand down that undeserved inheritance as undefiled as she received it.[245] Hence, the Book of Concord has attached to it a *Catalogue of Testimonies*, and such notable Lutherans as Chemnitz, Gerhard, and Flacius[246] wrote extensive works compiling patristic writings

---

[244]KW, Apology of the Augsburg Confession XXIV.1, 258.

[245]A. L. Barry, in the article previously quoted, "Lutheran Worship: Beyond 2000," writes: "Let us examine the flip side of this thesis. If Lutheran worship is a reflection of Lutheran theology, what do you think might happen if we were, for example, to begin to conduct our worship services in a manner similar to what one might find in a Baptist church, a Pentecostal church, or a non-denominational Evangelical church? Do you think it is reasonable to assume that if Lutherans worship like Baptists, it will probably not be too long before they believe as Baptists do? Or, if Lutherans worship like Charismatics, how long will it be before we embrace the doctrine and practices of the Charismatic movement? If we Lutherans recognize our roots and why we worship the way we do, it will probably also be true that we will wish to remain with that basic pattern of worship. As we contemplate changes in this pattern, we exercise restraint, care and caution, for we recognize that genuine Lutheran worship is a reflection of genuine Lutheran theology." http://worship.lcms.org/2000theses.html (accessed when I was in seminary, 2000–2004, it is no longer available at this address). It should be noted with respect to this A. L. Barry's observation above, however, that if Lutheran pastors and lay people are not educated in what worship really is and should strive to be (according to Scripture and the Lutheran Confessions), they will not appreciate the tradition that they have received from our fathers in the faith. A knowledge of church history, especially in the area of worship practices, will also only enhance our appreciation for why we do what we do. Catechesis, as in every area of the church's work, is essential.

[246]Oliver K. Olson writes: "Where Aldus collected the classics, Flacius, having embraced the Reformation, turned Europe upside down searching for medieval manuscripts. As an answer to the reproach that the Reformation

on contested doctrines—indeed, in many ways pioneered the field of patristics.[247] It was Carlstadt, not Luther, who gutted churches and rejected wholesale long-standing customs and ceremonies of the church. Luther, like the churches the Reformation inherited, left the majority of the Western Rite intact. Changes were made when the *lex credendi* required it (the canon of the Mass), when ceremonies were misunderstood or irreparably associated with papistic idolatry (the elevation of the host in some areas, the eucharistic prayer, etc.), and when a superior way of communicating the gospel was available (placement of the Words of Institution within the communion liturgy and their being spoken aloud). Luther and the subsequent confessors had anything but a scorched earth approach (such an approach, as Napoleon learned, seldom leaves one well-fed and grounded), where everything was to be destroyed and rebuilt from the foundation, as was the case to a large extent among the sects. Rather, as Charles Porterfield Krauth called it, theirs

---

was a break with the Catholic tradition of the church, he published texts from his researches in a *Catalog of Witnesses to the Truth*. He was confident that such historical records demonstrated that Luther's reform was faithful to the Catholic tradition. According to his 'remnant' argument, derived from 1 Kings 19:8 and Romans 11:4, there had always been a few faithful to the authentic tradition of the church. Catholicity, consequently, must be traced through the *successio doctrinae* rather than in the *successio personarum* of the 'historic episcopate.'" Oliver K. Olson, "Matthias Flacius," in *The Reformation Theologians: An Introduction to Theology in the Early Modern Period* (Oxford, Blackwell Publishers, 2001), 88. Notice that in Flacius' view catholicity is found first and foremost in teaching, not ritual. It is this catholic doctrine that will lead to truly catholic ritual, whether or not that ritual has widespread and longstanding precedent. Many widespread and longstanding rituals, however, are found to be vehicles of a very catholic *fides quae* and therefore worth preserving.

[247]The Lutheran Church confesses with the Augsburg Confession, "Since the churches among us do not dissent from the catholic church in any article of faith but only set aside a few abuses that are new and were accepted because of corruption over time contrary to the intention of the canons, we pray that Your Imperial Majesty will graciously hear about the changes and our reasons for them, so that people may not be compelled to observe these abuses against their conscience." KW, Augsburg Confession, Articles in Which an Account is Given of the Abuses that Have been Corrected 1, 61.

was "the conservative Reformation."[248] Chemnitz put it well in his *Examination of the Council of Trent*, Part II, "And indeed, for the sake of order and decorum it should not be permitted to everyone willfully, without the decision and consent of the church, just because he desires it, either to omit or change anything even in external and indifferent things."[249]

Freedom, while not free, as every crucifix ought to remind us, does however exist.[250] It is Christian freedom, though, and thus a

---

[248]Charles P. Krauth, *The Conservative Reformation and Its Theology* (Philadelphia: United Lutheran Publication House, 1871).

[249]Martin Chemnitz, *Examination of the Council of Trent, Part II*, trans. Fred Kramer (St. Louis: Concordia Publishing House, 1978), 108.

[250]Chemnitz writes about the freedom in ceremonies that existed also in the ancient church, which flies in the face of many a modern day liturgists who hold to the delusion of an utopian ancient liturgical community: "In the seventh place, the observance of these rites was free in the church; neither were such rites similar and the same in all churches; often also some of the most ancient rites were abrogated and omitted, such as the tasting beforehand of milk, honey, and wine, of which Tertullian and Jerome make mention. Some were changed and others newly instituted, as it was judged to serve the edification of the church. For the church used and preserved, not confused license but a godly and wholesome liberty in ecclesiastical ceremonies of this kind, instituted by men, so that by free discontinuance it abrogated, omitted, and changed also the most ancient such ceremonies when it was judged that by reason of circumstances they no longer were very important for piety, or when the cause for which they were first instituted and observed had either been removed or changed and they had thus ceased through the changed times to be useful for edification, or when they had turned aside from the purpose and use for which they had initially been instituted and had degenerated into abuse and superstition. But our opponents are delightful reformers who, when they have *ex professo* instituted a debate about ceremonies of this kind, do not with one word even make mention of these necessary reminders but only seek by their anathemas to burden the consciences, that at least the shadow of such rites, no matter what they are, which seem to have a certain pretext of custom in the Roman Church may be religiously observed, although now there is no true reason why they should be observed, no salutary purpose and use for edification; there are many such in the Canon of the Mass and in the ceremonies of Baptism, in the period of Easter and Pentecost." Chemnitz, *Examination of the Council of Trent, Part II*, 115.

freedom flowing from, grounded in, and governed by the gospel and Christian love, not a willy-nilly permit for frivolity.[251] Frivolity, as our Confessions, and I would hope common decency, make clear, has no place in God's services. As St. Paul warns, *"For you were called to freedom, brothers. Only do not use your freedom as an opportunity for the flesh, but through love serve one another."*[252] This freedom has existed from the earliest days of the Christian Church and will exist until Christ comes to rescue His Bride. *Ecclesia semper reformanda est*, and for that reason she has and must have the freedom and the responsibility to constantly adapt, improve and appropriate in each successive generation the traditions that have been passed onto it. Yet this adapting, improving, and appropriating, so necessary in every land and age, when it is done best and most rightly, however, will be done not on a whim and overnight, and not detached from the Church in the past or from the Church throughout the world, but thoughtfully, deliberately, and in accordance with and upon the foundation of the one infallible, unchanging, and salvific tradition: the Word. The Formula reminds us, first:

---

[251]Marquardt observes: "The a-liturgical orientation of our modern Reformed-pietistic environment moreover jumps only too easily to the conclusion that Article X simply consigns everything liturgical to the realm of *adiaphora*, so that as long as Word and sacraments still come to expression somehow, all outward arrangements are free and 'indifferent' That too would be a grave misunderstanding. The term *adiaphora* applies only to the strictly circumscribed area of external details neither commanded nor forbidden in God's Word. In no way does FC X abrogate Article XXIV of both the AC and the Apology, in which the Lutheran Church officially confesses its doctrinal stand on the nature of Christian worship—including such particulars as the divinely given relation between preaching and the sacrament (Ap XXIV, 33–40, 71–71, 80, 89), and the 'right use' of the historic Christian 'mass' (AC XXIV 35 German; Ap XXIV 74–77, 87). It would be a reductionist fallacy to confuse all such deeply theological issues with mere *adiaphora*." Kurt Marquardt, "Article X: The Formula of Concord: Confessions and Ceremonies," in *A Contemporary Look at the Formula of Concord* (St. Louis: Concordia Publishing House, 1978), 265–266.

[252]Galatians 5:13 ESV.

> For this reason the churches are not to condemn one another because of differences in ceremonies when in Christian freedom one has fewer or more than the other, as long as these churches are otherwise united in teaching and in all the articles of the faith as well as in the proper use of the holy sacraments. As it is said, *Dissonantia ieiunii non dissolvit consonantiam fidei*; (dissimilarity in fasting shall not destroy the unity of faith).[253]

And second:

> Therefore, we believe, teach, and confess that the community of God in every time and place has the right, power, and authority to change, reduce, or expand such practices according to the circumstances in an orderly and appropriate manner, without frivolity or offense, as seems most useful, beneficial, and best for good order, Christian discipline, evangelical decorum, and the building up of the church.[254]

Flacius' summary at the beginning of his great work on the subject of true and false adiaphora still serves us well:

> All ceremonies and church practices are in and of themselves as free as they will always be. When, however, coercion, the false illusion that they were worship of God and must be observed, renunciation [of the faith], offense, [or] an opening for godlessness develops, and when, in whatever way it may happen, they do not build up but rather tear down the church of God and mock God, then they are no longer adiaphora.[255]

Pastor Mark Schroeder, President of the Wisconsin Evangelical Lutheran Synod, succinctly stated the crux of the issue in his address to the 2009 convention of the synod, "In other words, when

---

[253]KW, Formula of Concord, Solid Declaration X.31, 640.

[254]KW, Formula of Concord, Solid Declaration X.9, 637.

[255]*Adiaphora and Tyranny*, 166.

something is determined to be an adiaphoron, that's not where the discussion *ends*; that is when discussion among Christians *begins*."[256]

Conversing, Confessing, Correcting, and Being Corrected as Brothers

Serious damage was done to the unity of Lutheranism in Germany, personal reputations, careers, and parish life by the controversies that developed after Luther's death and the Leipzig Interim. Some of this was inevitable, but not all of it. There is a great benefit in St. Paul's counsel, "Follow the pattern of the sound words that you have heard from me, in the faith and love that are in Christ Jesus."[257] In Christian freedom we have the freedom to adopt new or different theological language in order to express biblical truth, but in Christian love we do well to exercise caution in doing so. When there are misunderstandings concerning the meaning of theological terms, that is, regarding how a brother is using them, we do well to explore precisely how those involved are understanding the words under discussion.

We owe it to each other to speak clearly, and when we have spoken carelessly, intemperately, or without due clarity, to receive correction with humility and gratitude. There is no reason to persist in our carelessness, intemperateness, or lack of clarity. We have nothing to lose and everything to gain by growing in both our understanding and speech. Our brothers are gifts of God especially when they help us to grow in such a way. Our Lord Jesus deserves the best words and the most precise images and conceptions and we ought to want nothing less, both for His glory and for the benefit of His kingdom through the gospel properly preached and the

---

[256]This was part of his report to the 2009 convention in Saginaw, Michigan, the sixtieth biennial convention of the synod. The proceedings are available here: https://connect.wels.net/AOM/cop/2010%20District%20Conventions/Shared%20Documents/2009%20Proceedings.pdf (accessed December 28, 2015). The passage quoted is on page 102.

[257]2 Timothy 1:13 ESV.

gospel rightly administered. Let's not be defensive. Rather, let us with humility strive together to defend the clarity, beauty, and majesty of the Scriptures.

As brothers we also owe it to each other to realize that personalities can get into the way. We do well to take into consideration weaknesses in our own personalities as well as those of our brothers, and to work to overcome them. We do well to heed Luther's explanation to the Eighth Commandment, to be quick to forgive and quick to ask for forgiveness. Forgiveness is a powerful thing. Jesus knew that. As ambassadors of Christ, we do well to remember that as well.

We have an obligation to speak up for the truth, but we at the same time need not make quick recourse to polemics. We all have a little pope and a little Luther in us. We want to be the final authority and we want to take our stand at Worms. And yet God doesn't need popes and Lutheranism already had its Luther. God needs you to use your gifts in the places He places you in the ways that best edify His Church and benefit your neighbor. Your brother is your brother, not an enemy of Christ. He is a redeemed child of God, not the offspring of the devil. Remember his Baptism when you address him—the same Baptism with which you were baptized. Remember the Spirit who has bound us together as one. When a brother errs, labor to restore him in love, in a way that places no undo obstacle in the way of future reconciliation. Yes, there is a time for polemics, but that time is often not nearly as early in the process as we might assume.

That being said, it is perhaps good here to comment on the difference between public and private doctrine and practice as well as public and private sin. Sometimes I've read concerns about pubic discussions regarding public doctrine and practice. Not too long ago I read a pastor, sincerely, I am sure, advise that we should act like the confessors at Augsburg and choose to address almost all things in a private meeting. I didn't comment, but, I hope you know that is now how Augsburg worked, nor is it logistically possible. The confessors were summoned there to recant, in essence, but insisted upon presenting their faith, offering their heads before the Christian faith could be torn from their hearts. Imperial diets were few and far between, though. Lutherans did discuss doctrine and practice in the meanwhile. Luther certainly did. *Flugschriften* flew about. These things were fair game, although some discussed them unfairly. We need to strike a balance. We ought not be silenced into being silent about bad doctrine and practice. That is how orthodoxy is lost. Once again, though, we need to remember that we are not Luther, and our brother is not Erasmus or the pope, and the future of the gospel does not rest on our shoulders. There is a middle ground, and it is fraternal, even as it is frank. What does that look like? I could point to a number of Reformation pamphlets, but our time is limited. Ultimately, I trust that you, as my brothers, can feel it out and strive toward it.

Additionally, as we deal with each other, it is important to understand our brother's position correctly, and to strive to understand what has led him to hold it—what is he trying, often rightly, to preserve, although perhaps in the wrong way or with the wrong words? A surprising number of false teachings arise from a desire to protect some correct teaching. This was true even of many of the ancient heresies. Your brother did not necessarily set out to deny the truth of God when he spoke as he did. What is he trying to defend? What is his fear or concern? We can work together with great profit in order to address that fear and, in the process, we might even gain a better understanding for the biblical teaching the brother desires to defend and improve our own way of speaking about or understanding it. Thoughts do not spring from a vacuum. Endeavoring to discover why your brother is thinking what he is thinking is time well-spent and love well-shown. The major players in the "culture of controversy," largely because they shared a common Wittenberg education, often assumed that they all shared common presuppositions and theological emphases. They did not, and they didn't even think to consider the possibility that they operated with different starting points. We can easily make the same mistake. We share a common education, but that does not ensure that we always share and operate with the same presuppositions and emphases in our theological and ministerial labor. Some observations about the culture of conflict from Robert Kolb are perhaps pertinent for us today. Kolb writes:

> Most participants in the synergistic controversies had known each other from the time of their university studies, and they naturally presumed that their colleagues had understood their instructors just

> as they themselves had. Thus, these disputes were battles in a civil war, a *Bruderkrieg*; the participants had gotten acquainted as they listened to Luther and Melanchthon lecture at the Leucorea. Flacius, Gallus, Irenaeus, Pfeffinger, Strigel, Wigand, Marbach, Flinsbach, Spangenberg, and Chytraeus had studied in Wittenberg at roughly the same time, in the early 1540s; Selnecker, Kirchner, Chemnitz, Heshusius a decade later.[258]

I would add to this that both Melanchthon and Amsdorf had been dear friends of Luther and fellow members of the intimate Wittenberg circle that made reform possible. Brothers, there is much in this for us to consider. I pray the Lord Christ keeps us ever orthodox and true to His Word. If at all possible, I also pray that He ever keep us from unnecessary *Bruderkrieg*. Nothing is more bitter than a family feud, and many a family feud would end better if all involved remembered that they are family. How much more ought this be the case when we are family, not only by blood, but by Baptism—by blood, I suppose you could say, not that flows through our veins, but that flowed through the veins of God Himself. None of this is to say that we should compromise doctrine for a good ole *Kumbaya*. It simply means, when we must have it out, let's have it out as God would have us.

Scripture, Not as It Seems to You, but as It Is for You

Scripture says things, and it says them as God said them in Genesis 1, with a creative, formative purpose and power. Scripture is not ours to play with; no, we are Scripture's. Words mean things. The Word means things. He came, a real person, flesh and blood, was crucified, died, and was buried. Jesus is not an idea. He is not what we conceive of Him. He was conceived and born. He is, and so is His Word. His Word is bond. His promises cannot be thwarted, nuanced, or undone. We are captive to them. They take hold of us, not we them. And only disaster could and would result if it were not so. Through the Scriptures God makes chosen those He chose before the creation

[258]Kolb, *Bound Choice*, 277.

of the world. He takes the reins. He calms the sea. He does to us just what His Word says. Jesus comes to us as real as on Christmas, wrapped in the pages of our Bible and, specially, in the words of our preacher.

We are tempted in our day to speak of our interpretations of things. In this way, though, communication becomes both insincere and meaningless. Scripture is not the great American novel. We do not assign meaning to it. It has meaning. What matters is not what it means to us, but what it means *for us*. Scripture alone is the foundation and source of the Church's teaching and Scripture alone accomplishes what we cannot, for the Word acts through His Word. God might be hidden apart from His revelation, but in His revelation He is not hidden at all. He is there. The Scriptures do not need clarity, they are clear in and of themselves. Its words are not too simple to convey God's message. Rather, God's message is plain—and most beautiful—in the simple words of Scripture. While our old Adam loves to turn the issue on its head, the question isn't whether or not the Scriptures are clear, for they are, but rather whether the interpreter is.[259]

The Scriptures are not a tool. We don't take them up and do as we see fit. If anyone or anything is a tool, we are. The Scriptures lay hold of us. Yes, the Scriptures often come to us by the feet, in the hands, and through the mouths of another, but that another is a tool also. God is at work, through His Word, giving what His Word has done, doing what His Word promises and died and rose to deliver. We do ourselves and God a disservice when we forget that. God bought us with His Word. God placed His Word on us and buried us in it in Baptism. He feeds us with it in Holy Communion. He absolves us with it. God words His Word to us every day and it is by that Word alone that we live. The Word became Man and dwelt among us and by His Word He is with us still, delivering the benefits of His cross, claiming lame horses for His own—horses no one else in their right mind would claim. And so, may we, with the earliest Lutherans and with all believers of all time, confess what Isaiah first

---

[259]Gerhard O. Forde, *The Captivation of the Will: Luther vs. Erasmus on Freedom and Bondage* (Grand Rapids: William B. Eerdmans Publishing Company, 2005), 27.

declared and Peter echoed, not by compulsion, but willingly, because God's election, made our election through the gospel—has forced us to do so, against our will, but now most gladly in accord with it, torn as we are as sinner-saints. "The word of the Lord remains forever."[260] What is this word? "This word is the good news that was preached to you."[261] What will it do? "It shall not return to me empty."[262]

[260]Isaiah 40:8 ESV; 1 Peter 1:25 ESV.

[261]1 Peter 1:25 ESV.

[262]Isaiah 55:11 ESV.

Bibliography

Primary Sources

Amsdorff, Nicolaus von. *Auff Osianders Bekentnis ein Unterricht und zeugnis / Das sie Gerechtigkeit der menscheit Christi / darinnen sie entpfangen und geboren ist / allen Gleubigen Sündern geschanckt und zugerechent wird / und für ihr Person hie auff Erden nimmermehr Gerecht und heilig warden.* Magdeburg: Rödinger, 1552.

Amsdorff, Nicolaus von. *Epistolae Nicolai Amsdorfii et Martini Lutheri de Erasmo Roterodamo.* Wittenberg, 1534.

Amsdorff, Nicolaus von. *Ein kurtzer unterricht auff D. Georgen Maiors Antwort / das er nit unschüldig sey / wie er sich tragice rhümet.* Basel, 1552.

Bekenntnis Unterricht und vermanung der Pfarrhern und Prediger der Christlichen Kirchen zu Magdeburgk. Magdeburg: Michel Lotther, 1550.

Catechism of the Catholic Church. San Francisco, CA: Ignatius Press, 1994.

Chemnitz, Martin. *Examination of the Council of Trent.* Translated by Fred Kramer. Vol. 2. St. Louis: Concordia Publishing House, 1978.

Confessio et Apologia Pastorum & reliquorum ministrorum Ecclesiae Magdeburgensis. Magdeburg: Michaelem Lottherum, 1550.

Desiderius Erasmus. *In Praise of Folly.* Translated by Betty Radice. London: Penguin Books, 1994.

The English Standard Version Bible. New York: Oxford University Press, 2009.

Flacius Illyricus, Matthias. *Adiaphora and Tyranny.* Translated by Herbert C. Kuske and Wade R. Johnston. Saginaw, Michigan: Magdeburg Press, 2011.

Flacius Illyricus, Matthias. *Bericht M. Fla. Jllyrici, Von etlichen Artikeln der Christlichen Lehr, und von seinem Leben, und enlich auch von den Adiaphorischen Handlungen, wider die falschen Geticht der Adiaphoristen.* Jena: Thomas Rebart, 1559.

______. *Breves Summae Religionis Iesu Christi, & Antichristi.* Magdeburg: Michael Lotter, 1550.

______. *Clavis Scripturae Sacrae, seu de Sermone Sacrarum literarum.* Basileae: Ioannes Oporinus & Eusebius Episcopius, 1567.

______. Clavis Scripturae, seu de Sermone Sacrarum Literarum, plurimas generales Regulas continens. Altera Pars. Basel, 1567.

______. *Ein buch, von waren und falschen Mitteldingen, Darin fast der gantze handel von Mitteldingen erkleret wird, widder die schedliche Rotte der Adiaphoristen. Item ein brieff des ehrwirdigen Herrn D. Joannis Epini superintendenten zu Hamburg, auch von diesem handel an Illyricum geschrieben.* Magdeburg: Christian Rödinger, 1550.

______. *Eine Christliche vermanung zur bestendigkeit, inn der waren reinen Religion Jhesu Christi, unnd inn der Augsburgischen bekentnis. Geschrieben an die Meissnische Kirche, unnd andere, so das lauttere Evangelium Jhesu Christi erkant haben.* Magdeburg: Michael Lotter, 1550.

______. *Entschuldigung Matthiae Flacij Illyrici, geschrieben an die Universitet zu Wittemberg der Mittelding halben. Item sein brief an Philip. Melanthonem sampt etlichen andern schrifften dieselbige sach belangend. Verdeudscht.* Magdeburg: Christian Rödinger, 1549.

______. *Epistola S. Hulrici episcopi Augustani, circiter ante sexcentos et 50 annos, ad Pontificem Nicolaum primum, pro fefensone coniugii Sacerdotum, scripta, ex qua apparet, quam impudenter Papistae S. Patres jactent, cum et vita et doctrina cum S. Patribus plane ex Diametra pungent.* Magdeburg: Michael Lotter, 1549.

______. *Etliche Contradictiones . . . des Stenckfeldts daraus sein Geist leichtlich kan geprüfet warden.* Nürmnerg, 1556.

______. *Ein geistlicher trost dieser betrübten Magdeburigschen Kerchen Christi, das sie diese Verfolgung umb Gottes worts, und keiner andern ursach halben, leidet.* Magdeburg: Michael Lotter, 1551.

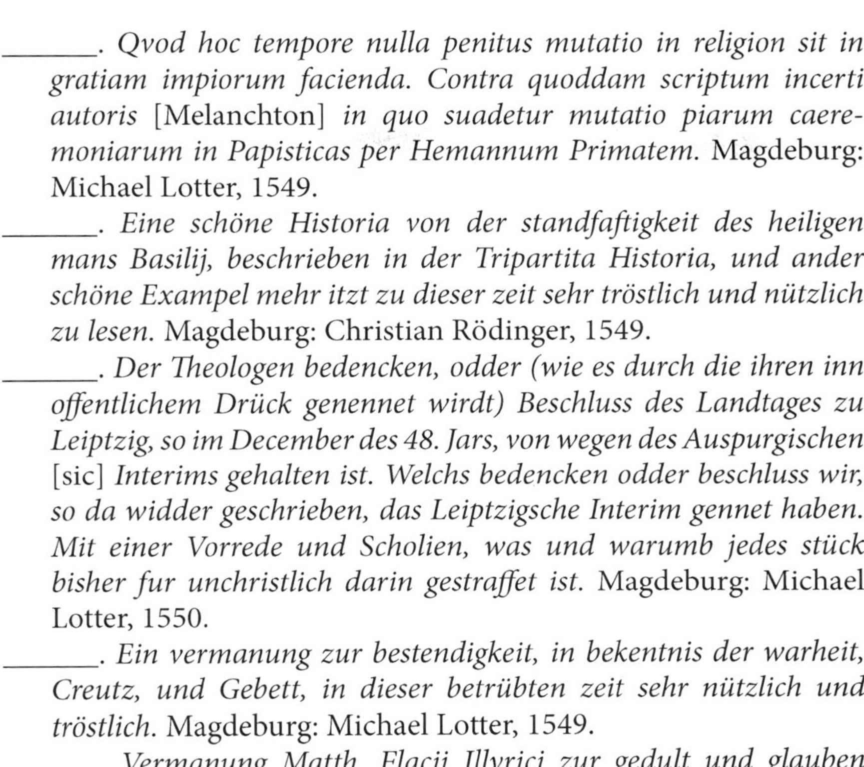

______. *Qvod hoc tempore nulla penitus mutatio in religion sit in gratiam impiorum facienda. Contra quoddam scriptum incerti autoris* [Melanchton] *in quo suadetur mutatio piarum caeremoniarum in Papisticas per Hemannum Primatem.* Magdeburg: Michael Lotter, 1549.

______. *Eine schöne Historia von der standfaftigkeit des heiligen mans Basilij, beschrieben in der Tripartita Historia, und ander schöne Exampel mehr itzt zu dieser zeit sehr tröstlich und nützlich zu lesen.* Magdeburg: Christian Rödinger, 1549.

______. *Der Theologen bedencken, odder (wie es durch die ihren inn offentlichem Drück genennet wirdt) Beschluss des Landtages zu Leiptzig, so im December des 48. Jars, von wegen des Auspurgischen* [sic] *Interims gehalten ist. Welchs bedencken odder beschluss wir, so da widder geschrieben, das Leiptzigsche Interim gennet haben. Mit einer Vorrede und Scholien, was und warumb jedes stück bisher fur unchristlich darin gestraffet ist.* Magdeburg: Michael Lotter, 1550.

______. *Ein vermanung zur bestendigkeit, in bekentnis der warheit, Creutz, und Gebett, in dieser betrübten zeit sehr nützlich und tröstlich.* Magdeburg: Michael Lotter, 1549.

______. *Vermanung Matth. Flacii Illyrici zur gedult und glauben zu Gott, im Creutz dieser verfolgung Geschrieben an die Kirche Christi zu Magdeburg.* Magdeburg: Christian Rödinger, 1551.

______. *Von fürnemlichem stücke / punct / order artikel der Schwenkfeldischen schwermerey.* Magdeburg, 1553.

Kolb, Robert and James A. Nestingen, eds. *Sources and Contexts of the Book of Concord.* Minneapolis: Fortress Press, 2001.

Kolb, Robert and Timothy J. Wengert, eds. *The Book of Concord: The Confessions of the Evangelical Lutheran Church.* Minneapolis: Fortress Press, 2000.

Luther, Martin. *The Bondage of the Will.* Edited by J. J. Packer and O. R. Johnston. Grand Rapids: Revell, 1957.

______. *Luthers Works, American Edition.* Edited by Jaroslav Pelikan and Helmut T. Lehman. 55 vols. Philadelphia: Fortress Press and St. Louis: Concordia Publishing House, 1955–1986.

Pfeffinger, Johannes. *De Libertate Voluntatis Humanae Quaestiones Quinque.* Leipzig: Gerorg Hantzsch, 1555.

Rupp, E. Gordon and Philip S. Watson, eds. *Luther and Erasmus: Free Will and Salvation*. Philadelphia: Westminster Press, 1969.

Secondary Sources

Arand, Charles P., Robert Kolb, and James A. Nestingen. *The Lutheran Confessions: History and Theology of the Book of Concord*. Minneapolis: Fortress Press, 2011.

Bainton, Roland. *Here I Stand: A Life of Martin Luther*. Nashville: Abingdon-Cokesbury Press, 1950.

Bente, F. *Historical Introductions to the Lutheran Confessions*, 2nd Ed. St. Louis: Concordia Publishing House, 2005.

Armand Boehme. "'But We've Always Done It That Way': Wittenberg and Canterbury on Tradition." *Logia: A Journal of Lutheran Theology* XII, nr. 4 (Reformation 2003): 11–17.

Brecht, Martin. *Martin Luther: His Road to Reformation, 1483–1521*. Translated by James L. Schaaf. Minneapolis: Fortress Press, 1993.

Brecht, Martin. *Martin Luther: Shaping and Defining the Reformation, 1521–1532*. Translated by James L. Schaaf. Minneapolis: Fortress Press, 1994.

Brecht, Martin. *Martin Luther: The Preservation of the Church, 1532–1546*. Translated by James L. Schaaf. Minneapolis: Fortress Press, 1999.

Christman, Robert J. *Doctrinal Controversy and Lay Religiosity in Late Reformation Germany. The Case of Mansfeld* [Studies in Medieval and Reformation Traditions]. Leiden: Brill, 2012.

______. "'*Wir sindt nichts den eytel sunde*': The Impact of Flacius' Theology of Original Sin on the German Territory of Mansfield." In Matija Vlačić Ilirik [III], 294–315. Labin: Grad Labin, 2012.

Deutschlander, Daniel M. *Grace Abounds: The Splendor of Christian Doctrine*. Milwaukee: Northwestern Publishing House, 2015.

______. *The Narrow Lutheran Middle: Following the Scriptural Road*. Milwaukee: Northwestern Publishing House, 2011.

______. *The Theology of the Cross: Reflections on His Cross and Ours*. Milwaukee: Northwestern Publishing House, 2008.

Dingel, Irene, ed. *Der Adiaphoristische Streit (1548–1560).* [Controversia et Confessio. Theologische Kontroversen 1548–1577/1580: Kritische Auswahledition. Vol. 2]. Göttingen: Vandenhoeck & Ruprecht, 2010.

______. "Bekenntnis und Geschichte: Funktion und Entwicklung des reformatischen Bekenntnisses im 16. Jahrhundert." In *Dona Melanchthoniana: Festgabe für Heinz Scheible zum 70. Geburtstag*, edited by Johanna Loehr, 61–81. Stuttgart: Evangelische Friedrich Frommann Verlag, 2001.

______. *Concordia controversa: Die öffentlichen Diskussionen um das lutherische Konkordienwerk am Ende des 16. Jahrhunderts.* Göttingen: Gütersloher Verlagshaus, 1996.

______. "The Culture of Conflict in the Controversies Leading to the Formula of Concord (1548–1560)." In *Lutheran Ecclesiastical Culture, 1550–1675*, edited by Robert Kolb, 15–64. Leiden: Brill, 2008.

______. "Flacius als Schüler Luthers und Melanchthons." In *Vestigia Pietatis. Studien zur Geschichte der Frömmigkeit in Thüringen und Sachsen*, edited by Gerhard Graf, Hans-Peter Hasse, and Ernst Koch, 77–93. Leipzig: Evangelische Verlagsanstalt, 2000.

______, ed. *Reaktionen auf das Augsburger Interim: Der Interimistische Streit (1548–1549).* [Controversia et Confessio. Theologische Kontroversen 1548–1577/1580: Kritische Auswahledition. Vol. 2]. Göttingen: Vandenhoeck & Ruprecht GmbH & Co., 2010.

Dingel, Irene and Günther Wartenberg, eds. *Politik und Bekenntnis: Die Reaktionen auf das Interim von 1548.* Leipzig: Evangelische Verlagsanstalt, 2006.

Englebert, Omer. *The Lives of the Saints.* Translated by Christopher and Anne Fremantle. New York: Barnes and Noble, 1994.

Forde, Gerhard O. *On Being a Theologian of the Cross: Reflections on Luther's Heidelberg Disputation, 1518.* Grand Rapids, Michigan: Wm. B. Eerdmans, 1997.

______. *The Captivation of the Will: Luther vs. Erasmus on Freedom and Bondage.* Grand Rapids: William B. Eerdmans Publishing Company, 2005.

Giertz, Bo. *The Hammer of God.* Translated by Clifford Ansgar Nelson and Hans Andrae. Minneapolis: Augsburg Books, 2005.

Haug-Moritz, Gabriele. *Der Schmalkaldische Bund, 1530–1541/42.* Leinfelden-Echterdingen: DRW-Verlag Weinbrenner GmbH & Co., 2002.

Hendrix, Scott H. *Martin Luther: Visionary Reformer.* New Haven: Yale University Press, 2015.

Ilić, Luka. "'*Der Heilige Man und thewre held*': Flacius' View of Luther." In Matija Vlačić Ilirik [III], 294–315. Labin: Grad Labin, 2012.

______. *Theologian of Sin and Grace: The Process of Radicalization in the Theology of Matthias Flacius Illyricus.* Göttingen: Vandenhoeck & Ruprecht, 2014.

Thomas Kaufmann, *Das Ende der Reformation* (Tübingen: Mohr Siebeck, 2003)

Kaufmann, Thomas. *Das Ende der Reformation.* Tübingen: Mohr Siebeck, 2003.

______. *Konfession und Kultur.* Tübingen: Mohr Siebeck, 2006.

______. "Matthias Flacius Illyricus. Lutherischer Theologe und Magdeburer Publizist." In *Mitteldeutsche Lebensbilder: Menschen im Zeitalter der Reformation*, edited by Werner Freitag, 177–200. Köln: Böhlau Verlag, 2004.

______. "'Our Lord God's Chancery' in Magdeburg and Its Fight against the Interim." *Church History* 73, no. 3 (September 2004): 566–582.

Kittelson, James M. *Luther the Reformer: The Story of the Man and His Career.* Minneapolis: Fortress Press, 1986.

Klann, R. "Article I. Original Sin." In *A Contemporary Look at the Formula of Concord*, edited by Wilbert Rosin and Robert Preus, 103–121. St. Louis: Concordia Publishing House, 1978.

Koelpin, A. J. "Luther's Theology of the Cross." Paper presented at Dr. Martin Luther College, New Ulm, MN. 1981. In Wisconsin Lutheran Seminary Essay File, http://www.wlsessays.net/bitstream/handle/123456789/2604/Luther%27s%20Theology%20of%20the%20Cross.pdf?sequence=1&isAllowed=y (accessed December 21, 2015).

Kolb, Robert. *Bound Choice, Election, and Wittenberg Theological Method.* Grand Rapids: William B. Eerdmans Publishing Company, 2005.

______, ed. *Lutheran Ecclesiastical Culture, 1550–1675*. Leiden: Brill, 2008.

______. *Martin Luther as Prophet, Teacher, and Hero: Images of the Reformer, 1520–1620*. Grand Rapids, MI: Baker Books, 1999.

______. *Martin Luther: Confessor of the Faith*. [Christian Theology in Context]. Oxford: Oxford University Press, 2009.

Kolb, Robert, Irene Dingel, and L'umbomír, eds. *The Oxford Handbook of Martin Luther's Theology* (Oxford: Oxford University Press, 2014).

Krauth, Charles P. *The Conservative Reformation and Its Theology*. Philadelphia: United Lutheran Publication House, 1871.

Lindberg, Carter. *The European Reformations*. 2nd Ed. Malden, Massachusetts: Blackwell, 2010.

______, ed. *The Reformation Theologians: An Introduction to Theology in the Early Modern Period*. Oxford: Blackwell, 2002.

MacCulloch, Diarmaid. *The Reformation: A History*. New York: Penguin Books, 2005.

Marquardt, Kurt. "Article X. Confession and Ceremonies." In *A Contemporary Look at the Formula of Concord*, edited by Wilbert Rosin and Robert D. Preus, 260–270. St. Louis: Concordia Publishing House, 1978.

_____. "'Church Growth' as Mission Paradigm: A Confessional Lutheran Assessment." In *Church and Ministry Today: Three Confessional Lutheran Essays*, edited by John A. Maxfield, 51–172. St. Louis: Luther Academy, 2001.

Meyer, John. *Studies in the Augsburg Confession*. Milwaukee: Northwestern Publishing House, 1995.

Moritz, Anja. *Interim und Apokalypse*. Tübingen: Mohr Siebeck, 2009.

Nelson, Clifford E. *The Lutherans in North America*. Philadelphia: Fortress Press, 1975.

Nestingen, James A. *Martin Luther: A Life*. Minneapolis: Fortress Press, 2003.

Nietzsche, Friedrich. *Beyond Good and Evil*. Translated by Marion Faber. Oxford: Oxford World's Classics, 2008.

______. *The Will to Power*. Translated by Walter Kaufmann and R. J. Hollingdale. New York: Vintage Books, 1967.

Oberman, Heiko A. *Luther: Man between God and the Devil.* New York: Image Books, 1992.

Olson, Oliver K. *Matthias Flacius and the Survival of Luther's Reform.* Wiesbaden, Germany: Harrassowitz Verlag, 2002.

______. "Matthias Flacius (1520–1575)." In *The Reformation Theologians: An Introduction to the Early Modern Period*, edited by Carter Lindberg, 83–93. Oxford: Blackwell, 2002.

______. *Reclaiming the Lutheran Liturgical Heritage.* Minneapolis: Bronze Bow Publishing, 2007.

______. "Theology of Revolution: Magdeburg, 1550–1551." *The Sixteenth Century Journal* 3, no. 1 (April 1972): 56–79.

Paulson, Steven D. *Lutheran Theology.* New York: T&T Clark International, 2011.

______. "A Royal Ass." Paper presented at Lutheran Free Conference, Martin Luther College, New Ulm, MN. November 6–7, 2013.

______. "What Is Essential in Lutheran Worship." *Word & World* 26, nr. 1 (Spring 2006): 149–161.

Pettegree, Andrew. *Brand Luther.* New York: Penguin Press, 2015.

Preger, Wilhelm. *Matthias Flacius Illyricus und seine Zeit.* 2 vols. Erlangen: T. Bläsing, 1859–1861.

Preus, Robert D., ed. *A Contemporary Look at the Formula of Concord.* St. Louis: Concordia Publishing House, 1978.

Rein, Nathan. *The Chancery of God: Protestant Print, Polemic and Propaganda against the Empire, Magdeburg 1546–1551.* Burlington, Vermont: Ashgate, 2008.

______. "Faith and Empire: Conflicting Visions of Religion in a Late Reformation Controversy—The Augsburg *Interim* and Its Opponents, 1548–1550." *Journal of the American Academy of Religion* 71, no. 1 (March 2003): 45–74.

Sasse, Hermann. *We Confess Anthology.* Translated by Norman Nagel. Saint Louis: Concordia Publishing House, 1999.

Schalk, Carl F. "Hymnody and the Proclamation of the Gospel." In *Not Unto Us: A Celebration of the Ministry of Kurt J. Eggert*, edited by William H. Braun and Victor H. Prange, 129–139. Milwaukee: Northwestern Publishing House, 2001.

Schorn-Schütte, Luise, ed. *Das Interim 1548/50.* Heidelberg: Verein für Reformationsgeschichte, 2005.

Skinner, Quentin. *The Age of Reformation.* Vol. 2 of *The Foundations of Modern Political Thought.* Cambridge: Cambridge University Press, 1978.

Spitz, Lewis W. and Wenzel Lohff. *Discord, Dialogue, and Concord: Studies in the Lutheran Reformation's Formula of Concord.* Philadelphia: Fortress Press, 1977.

Steinmetz, David C. *Luther in Context.* 2nd Ed. Grand Rapids: Baker Academic, 2002.

———, *Reformers in the Wings: From Geiler von Kaysersberg to Theodore Beza.* 2nd Ed. Oxford: Oxford University Press, 2001.

Schwiebert, E. G. *Luther and His Times: The Reformation from a New Perspective.* St. Louis: Concordia Publishing House, 1950.

Tiefel, James P. "The Formation and Flow of Worship Attitudes in the Wisconsin Evangelical Lutheran Synod" In *Not Unto Us: A Celebration of the Ministry of Kurt J. Eggert*, edited by William H. Braun and Victor H. Prange, 141–165. Milwaukee: Northwestern Publishing House, 2001.

Walther, C. F. W. *Law and Gospel: How to Read and Apply the Bible.* Translated by Christian C. Tiews. St. Louis: Concordia Publishing House, 2010.

Wentz, Abdel Ross. *A Basic History of Lutheranism in America.* Philadelphia: Muhlenberg Press, 1955.

Whitford, David M. *Tyranny and Resistance: The Magdeburg Confession and the Lutheran Tradition.* St. Louis: Concordia Publishing House, 2001.

Index

Notes are indicated by *n* after the page number.

60567976R00071

Made in the USA
Lexington, KY
10 February 2017